NATIVE FOODS celebration COOKBOOK

delicious vegan recipes to
celebrate every month of the year!

Book One: The Native Foods Cookbook Series

Printed in China

Publisher's Cataloging-in-Publication
(Provided by Quality Books, Inc.)

Native foods celebration cookbook : delicious vegan recipes
  to celebrate every month of the year.
    pages cm. -- (The native foods cookbook series ; book 1)
    Includes index.
    LCCN 2013951737
    ISBN 978-0-9910179-0-4
    eISBN 978-0-9910179-1-1

   1. Vegan cooking. 2. Cookbooks.   I. Series: Native
foods cookbook series ; bk. 1.

TX837.N38 2013   641.5′636
                             QBI13-600176

Book Cover Design: Sarah K. Young
Interior Book Design and Layout: AuthorsTeam.com

Recipes for Cover Photos:
  Front Cover:
    Summer in Asia Roll p.139
    Cantaloupe Martini p.205
    Verdi's Roasted Veggie Pizza p.287
    Shroom Burger p.147
    Pina Colada Popsicles p.191
  Back Cover:
    Raw Key Lime Parfait p.157
    Seitan "Coq" Au Vin p.229

ACKNOWLEDGMENTS

- To our wonderful guests and cookbook readers, whose passion for our food and our mission inspire us to keep feeding, creating and growing. Your support has truly made this book (and so much more!) possible. So keep coming hungry!

- To Andrea McGinty (Co-owner), who truly believes we can change the world with something as simple as our forks. Dissatisfied by the options her young daughter was presented in the name of healthy food, she took her love of a plant-based diet and vowed to share it with the rest of the world. Her vision for Native Foods Café and the future of food as fun, fresh, healthy and delicious has spread the love of veganism far and wide. And if that's not enough, to Andrea, for enthusiastically leading this project and giving us all a few more reasons to celebrate.

- To Lauren Neuschel (Lead Writer), for her original, vibrant writing and aptitude for design. The long hours she spent at her computer and at photo shoots give this cookbook its color and character.

- To Sammy Caiola (Assistant Writer), for her creative voice, keen edits and endless supply of foodie puns. And for knocking out witty copy when the going got tough.

- To our Culinary Team and Executive Chefs, whose culinary talent, innovative cuisine and attention to detail filled this book with top-notch creations.

- To the Wicker Park staff, for being so hospitable to the group of photographers and curious customers hanging around the Starving Artist's Gallery during weeks of photo shoots. The happy, fun vibe and soft afternoon light in the restaurant were just what we needed.

- To Jacqueline Lange, owner of 400 cookbooks and major foodie. Her commentary and acute palette were extremely helpful for getting these recipes just right.

- To Allette Daley, for being the home kitchen tester and helping us tweak the food to perfection.

- To Julius Balcerak, who tirelessly helped us with every request along the way.

TABLE OF CONTENTS

INTRODUCTION

Welcome to the Native Foods Celebration Cookbook!

The first rule of thumb here at Native Foods Café is to love your food… like really love your food, inside and out. We love the scent of lemongrass tofu floating out from our kitchen and the taste of garlic-roasted veggies fresh off the grill. We love sharing delicious plant-based meals with the people we love, and introducing friends who are ready to take on a new culinary adventure.

So why are we so passionate? We truly believe we can change the world with one simple tool: our forks. Every meal you eat is a bite into the future of your health, and with this book we're opening minds (and mouths!) to food that's rich in flavor, texture and ethnic flair. Who knew that something as simple as a fork could launch us in a positive direction in the name of our health, the Earth and our animal friends?

We did. So we say, "Long live the fork!"

Plant-based cooking is exploding. It's innovative. And it's becoming the center of the plate for food lovers everywhere. Vegan cuisine is here to stay, and it's so much easier than it used to be. It's popping up on grocery shelves, sliding down cafeteria lines, infiltrating restaurant menus and showing off on dining room tables. With all of the buzz, an increasingly diverse community is tuning in to our health-happy (and taste bud approved!) cuisine.

So what brings you here? Perhaps your kids are talking about moving Meatless Mondays from their school cafeteria to the dinner table. Maybe you're itching to get back into those skinny jeans, or ready to start training for your first 5k. Flexitarian, pescatarian, vegan, undecided, or unaffiliated—this cookbook is for you. Our recipes aim to please palates, make you feel good and make the transition to a whole foods diet effortless. People often ask what "Native Foods" means; what makes our food "native"? Simply put, the food we prepare comes from the earth and goes straight to our plates!

It all started in 1994, when one passionate chef with a commitment to animal welfare opened the first Native Foods Café in Palm Springs, California. Now we're sprouting up all over the country serving fun, fresh and unique dishes. Our goal is to change the way people think about food. We are incredibly grateful to those who have helped us grow over the years, and cannot wait to share plant-based power with the rest of the world.

Until then, we'd love for people to share our recipes in the comfort of their own homes. And we know every home has its celebrations and traditions involving food, whether it is an uncle's signature eggnog, or a great grandma's stuffing. The recipes in this book are based on those traditions, but with a creative, plant-based twist. You'll be pleasantly surprised by how easy it is to recreate holiday classics with no meat or dairy whatsoever. All it takes is a little prep and a whole lot of love. No matter what you're celebrating—from a New Year's brunch to an all-out barbeque—you'll find just what you need to please the palates of vegetarians and omnivores alike.

For years, we've been cooking with the seasons and building menus that help communities celebrate the Native way. So in an effort to catapult our love of vegan cuisine outside of our restaurants and into your home, we're dishing some of our best and tastiest recipes. We've had a blast creating these dishes and we hope they inspire you and yours towards a more sustainable and healthful lifestyle. And if nothing more, let them become your guide to some seriously good eats. Pass the food around the table, bring it to work, and pack it in a picnic basket. Plant-based cooking is so easy that you can use it for special occasions *and* your daily routine. Now that's something to celebrate!

VEGAN PANTRY

Level One

So you've got the cookbook. Now it's time to stock your pantry for a fun, fresh, culinary adventure. Don't worry! This doesn't mean your kitchen is going to transform into a maze of unfamiliar ingredients and oddly shaped bottles. There are tons of tasty treats you can make with just a few vegan-specific items, many of which are available at your neighborhood grocery store. These first ten are affordable, pronounceable and multipurpose. So don't stress about the new ingredients breaking your bank, or running to a dozen health stores each week. Grab these key ingredients and you'll be ready to roll like a real Native Foods' chef.

1. Non-dairy milk
2. Grains
3. Nutritional yeast
4. Vegan mayo
5. Nuts and seeds
6. Beans
7. Vegan butter
8. Apple cider vinegar
9. Coconut oil
10. Cornstarch

Level Two

The following ingredients really are nice additions, as they will allow you to whip up sauces, dressings and baked goods in a pinch. From silken tofu to dried mushrooms, these are the tricks of the trade that will have even the toughest carnivores asking for seconds. And the good news is (again!) you probably already have a few of these hanging around the kitchen.

1. Organic sugar
2. Canned tomatoes
3. Silken tofu
4. Unbleached flour
5. Pasta
6. Dijon mustard
7. Dried mushrooms
8. Olive oil
9. Vegetable broth
10. Apple sauce

Level Three

Ever wonder how Native Foods creates its mouthwatering, flavor-packed cuisine without harming a single animal? It takes a lot of love, a little bit of magic, and a few extra ingredients. Creating vegan food that isn't just palatable, but is downright addicting, requires some specialized items.

1. Agar agar
2. Balsamic vinegar
3. Vital wheat gluten
4. Miso paste
5. Agave
6. Capers
7. Vegan cream cheese
8. Liquid aminos
9. Chickpea flour
10. Tahini

GLOSSARY

Level One

Non-dairy milks: Did you know that humans are the only species that drinks another animal's milk? At Native Foods, we opt for healthier, more natural alternatives to dairy by using soy, rice or almond milk. For a sweeter flavor, try coconut or hazelnut milk. You'll find non-dairy milk in most grocery stores.

Grains (quinoa, millet, buckwheat): Grains are a great accompaniment to vegetable-based recipes like bowls and stir-fries, and can also be used in burgers and baked goods. Quinoa is a quickly-cooking, high-protein grain that grows naturally in three beautiful colors: red, black and gold. Millet is a great source of magnesium that's used in everything from polenta to pancakes. You won't believe the possibilities that open up when you think outside of the rice box.

Nutritional yeast: These savory flakes are a huge source of Vitamin B12 and the magic ingredient behind our non-dairy cheese. The yeast makes a great substitute for parmesan, so toss it on a salad (or popcorn) and let your taste buds go wild.

Vegan Mayonnaise: This mayonnaise substitute works wonders when jazzing up a vegan sandwich, and is now available in pesto, chipotle, tartar sauce, horseradish, BBQ and roasted garlic flavors.

Nuts and Seeds: When settling into a plant-based diet, you'll want to keep a full stock of nuts and seeds for cooking. We make frequent use of cashews and almonds in our recipes, but chestnuts, hazelnuts, walnuts and pecans are also great to have on hand. Plus, they help make delicious, dairy-free cheese. When it comes to seeds, sunflower and pumpkin are our favorites.

Beans: Beans are a key source of protein that give a warm, hearty flavor to plant-based meals. We like white beans, black beans, garbanzo beans, kidney beans, navy beans, pinto beans … heck, we love em' all! Dried varieties are convenient, economical and long lasting, so be sure to keep some stocked up.

Vegan butter or shortening: While oils are best for cooking, you'll also need a spread with a buttery flavor for a lot of our baked goods and casseroles. A variety of vegan butters and shortening—made from a blend of natural oils—are readily available and perfect for your vegan cooking needs.

Apple cider vinegar: We like this vinegar for its subtle flavor and slight acidic bite. It reacts with baking soda to help pastries rise, giving them a soft, airy quality. Plus, its long list of health benefits includes stronger teeth and hair, lower cholesterol and a more resistant immune system.

Coconut oil: No chef should go without the light and fragrant coconut oil. It can be used for baking, or to add a sweet touch to curries and salsas. It's known to speed up metabolism and increase energy, so add a drop to your dish and a pep to your step.

Cornstarch: Similar to arrowroot, this starchy yellow powder makes a great thickener for soups, sauces and desserts and is a staple for breads and pancakes. It's totally vegan, but stick with organic and non-GMO varieties, as the starch is extracted from farm-grown corn.

Level Two

Organic sugar: Contrary to popular belief, not all sugar is vegan. Many bleached sugars use an animal bone product to attain their white color. We use organic cane sugar, which has a high molasses content and a darker color. You'll find cane sugar at most grocery stores.

Canned tomatoes: You can't go wrong with a can of this delicious red fruit around the house. It's economical. It's quick. And it's 100% vegan. Incorporate it into pizza sauce, pasta, curry, soup and much more. Just be sure to keep an eye out for BPA-free cans.

Silken tofu: This soft tofu variety is the kind you'll find in some miso soups, but can also be used for cooking and baking. Find it in the refrigerated section of most grocery stores in a rectangular, plastic package or on the shelf in the international section. Make sure you drain it before use, and explore all the dishes you can make with its smooth, velvety texture.

Unbleached flour: Like sugar, flour isn't always vegan. Look for unbleached, organic varieties.

Eggless pasta: Pasta can be a lifesaver when you need carbs in a pinch. Always keep a few eggless varieties on hand—all shapes and sizes are welcome!

Dijon mustard: This zesty condiment makes an appearance in many of our recipes, always ready to add a kick to a salad or stew.

Dried mushrooms: Mushroom lovers delight in the dried variety, which is economical and lasts for ages. Reconstitute these mushrooms and use them for cooking at your leisure. Don't worry—they still maintain their bold, savory flavor after the drying process.

Olive oil: Most of our recipes use olive oil, which is packed with nutrients and earthy flavors that enrich vegan cuisine. Use 'virgin' for cooking and 'extra-virgin' as a condiment.

Vegetable broth: This hearty liquid is a key flavoring agent in several of our recipes. Keep a healthy supply in your cabinet and you'll never go hungry again. Tip: It'll taste even better if you make it yourself.

Apple sauce: With eggs out of the picture, applesauce can be a big help for making moist vegan baked goods and can also be used for sauces and chutneys.

Level Three

Agar agar: Gelatin and marshmallows may look harmless, but their squishy, fluffy composures come from the hooves of thousands of horses, pigs and cows. Instead use agar, a gelatin substitute derived from a variety of East Asian seaweeds. Agar comes in flakes and powder and can be used as a thickener for custards and other sweets.

Balsamic vinegar: This vinegar originates from the pressings of white Trebbiano grapes that never fermented. As it ages, its texture becomes thicker and its flavor more complex. Use it in dressings and sauces and to bring out fruits like raspberries, strawberries and peaches. Find it in most grocery stores.

Vital wheat gluten: Meet gluten: wheat's most abundant natural protein. Vital wheat gluten is the powdered form of gluten, which is high in protein and useful for making stretchy dough and fantastic breads. It is also a key ingredient in a meat substitute called seitan (see protein section).

Miso paste: Made from fermented soybeans, this Japanese paste comes in handy for soups, marinades and dressings. It's high in salt and Vitamin B.

Agave nectar: This amber liquid, extracted from the agave cactus of Mexico, makes a great alternative to sugar and honey and is extremely useful when concocting vegan desserts.

Capers: You'd probably imagine that eating a flower would be sweet, but these flower buds are actually quite salty. They come from a Mediterranean plant that, when pickled, takes on a briny, lemony flavor similar to an olive. They work well on salads and sandwiches and are available at most grocery stores.

Vegan Cream Cheese: Another refrigerator staple, vegan cream cheese works well in desserts and baked goods. Spread it on toast in the morning, or try it in some of our festive dips.

Liquid Aminos: Similar to soy sauce, but with an extra special zing! Use it as a substitute for soy sauce and tamari.

Chickpea Flour: Chickpeas are a big hit in vegan cooking, and their flour is no exception. Chickpea flour is gluten-free and can do all the same things as regular flour. It has a slightly nuttier flavor and yellower color, but it's much higher in protein and great to have on hand.

Tahini: This smooth, creamy butter is made from ground sesame seeds and is excellent for Mediterranean and South Asian dishes. *And* it's rich in protein and calcium!

Protein Central

Tempeh: Tempeh originated in Indonesia and is made from cultured soybeans and millet. It has a light nutty flavor and is rich in protein, iron and antioxidants.

Seitan: Seitan is also known as "wheat meat." It is made by kneading and rinsing wheat flour until all the starch is removed and it becomes a pure protein. It has a delicate, meaty texture, and it's delicious!

Firm Tofu: Tofu is made from soybeans, water and a curdling agent. It comes in white blocks and absorbs any flavors around it. There are firm and extra firm varieties, which can be cubed and added to any scramble or stir fry. It's basically a vegan's best friend.

What's all that other mumbo jumbo?

Making a "roux": In a lot of our recipes, we make a roux to help thicken sauces or soups. The French-ness of the word makes it sound complicated, but it's actually pretty easy. Just melt vegan butter in a saucepan, until it turns frothy. Then use a whisk to stir in an equal weight of unbleached organic flour. (One ounce of butter calls for one ounce of flour.) Keep stirring until a paste forms, and there you have it!

Shocking a vegetable in an "ice bath": In this case, "shocking" is just another word for "refreshing." We throw vegetables in an ice bath just after blanching to stop the cooking and preserve all of the flavor and color. Plus it makes entertaining even easier— make your vegetables ahead of time, shock them and then reheat come party time.

How to "zest" a lime or lemon: The rind of a lime and lemon packs so much flavor that we never just throw them away. To capture the rind, rub the lime or lemon on all sides against a microplane over a cutting board, (just as you would a block of vegan cheese), until all of the rind is removed. It's easy peasy, lemon squeeze-y.

NEW YEAR, NATIVE YOU

- BKT Omelet
- Mulberry Farm Scones
- El Benedicto Ranchero
- Spicy Bloody Harry
- Twice-Baked Savory Breakfast Cakes
- Oh Mama! Italian Breakfast Pizza
- Blueberry Thrill Cobbler

The New Year starts with fireworks and a little bubbly at late-night parties from coast to coast. Chances are nothing sounds better after a sparkling night out than a savory and satisfying breakfast in.

If you're hosting brunch on the first—and let's face it, by the time you and your guests roll out of bed it's probably lunch—then you'll likely want a no-hassle kind of meal. The following recipes are easy to prepare ahead of time in case you need a little time to recover.

We realize it can feel like the celebrations are over just as the new year starts, but heck, we still have the rest of this book to celebrate! But before we get too ahead of ourselves, savor today first. Relax and enjoy—everyone knows January 2nd is the first *real* day of the year.

BKT OMELET

See it in a sandwich, throw it in an omelet. That's our motto. And our BKT (kale rules!)—a take on the classic BLT—might just become part of your morning routine.

RECIPE
Serves 4 to 6

"EGG" BATTER

2 cloves	garlic, pressed	½ tsp.	sea salt
14 ounces	silken tofu	½ cup	chickpea flour
2 tbsp.	nutritional yeast	⅛ tsp.	onion powder
½ tsp.	turmeric	⅛ tsp.	smoked paprika

Mix all ingredients together in a blender and blend until smooth.

ROASTED CHERRY TOMATOES

1 pint	cherry tomatoes	½ tsp.	pepper
2 tbsp.	olive oil	½ tsp.	parsley, chopped
1 tsp.	sea salt		

1. Toss cherry tomatoes with olive oil. Place on baking sheet.
2. Sprinkle with remaining ingredients and roast in the oven at 500°F for about 2 to 3 minutes.

ASSEMBLY

1 recipe	"Egg" Batter	1 cup	mushrooms, sliced and sautéed
1 cup	vegan mozzarella		
1 recipe	Roasted Cherry Tomatoes	1 recipe	Native Bacon (page 23), chopped into bacon bits
1 cup	kale, steamed and chopped		

13

1. Preheat a large non-stick sauté pan over medium-high heat.
2. Add ½ cup of the omelet batter into the skillet. Spread the batter out into about a 6-inch circle.
3. Let it cook for 1 to 3 minutes before flipping. The top of the omelet should dry and become a dull matte yellow when ready to flip.
4. Fill the omelet with the cheese, tomatoes, kale, mushrooms and Native Bacon. Then heat in the oven on a baking sheet at 350°F for about 4 minutes.

ROASTED POTATOES

1 pound	Yukon Gold potatoes, cut into 1-inch cubes	1 tsp.	ground black pepper
1 tsp.	sea salt	5 cloves	garlic
1 pound	sweet potatoes, cut into 1-inch cubes	4 sprigs	rosemary
		¼ cup	olive oil

1. Place all ingredients in a mixing bowl and mix well.
2. Place on a sheet pan and bake in the oven at 350°F for about 15 to 20 minutes, turning once.
3. Remove from heat, remove rosemary sprigs and let cool.

MULBERRY FARM SCONES

We're smitten with these simple delights. What could be homier for New Year's Day parade watching than freshly baked scones? Our favorite part of the recipe besides the perfectly tart mulberries? The instructions that say to drop "generous" spoonfuls of batter onto the pan.

RECIPE

Serves 10

1 cup	unbleached organic flour	1 ½ tsp.	vanilla extract
1 tsp.	baking powder	⅓ cup	water
½ tsp.	sea salt	½ cup	soy or rice milk
2 tbsp.	organic sugar	½ cup	dry mulberries (rehydrate in
3 tbsp.	coconut oil, melted		2 cups hot water, strain)

1. Preheat oven to 400°F.
2. In a medium bowl, mix together flour, baking powder and salt.
3. In a separate bowl, mix the organic sugar, coconut oil, vanilla extract, water and rice or soy milk. Stir in flour mixture alternating with the mulberries, a little at a time, until just combined. Do not over mix; batter will be thick.
4. Drop generous spoonfuls onto a greased baking pan. Bake 15 to 18 minutes or until edges begin to turn golden.

EL BENEDICTO RANCHERO

'**E**ggs' Benedict (with a ranchero twist!) is one of those breakfast masterpieces. A true Picasso. And if a *vegan* recipe can conquer eggs, Hollandaise Sauce *and* chorizo all in one dish, then it must be a fine piece of art indeed.

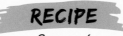

RECIPE
Serves 6

VEGETABLE STOCK
Makes 2 ½ cups

½ cup	onions, diced	1 cup	celery, diced
1 cup	carrots, diced	1 tsp.	whole black peppercorns
½ cup	red peppers, diced	3 whole	bay leaves
6 cloves	garlic	1 ½ quarts	water
¼ cup	button mushrooms, diced		

1. Place everything in a medium to large-sized stockpot and bring to a slow boil.
2. Once boiled, reduce heat to a low simmer. Allow stock to slowly simmer and seep up vegetable juices for at least one hour or until reduced by half.
3. Strain vegetables out using a colander or strainer. (You won't need the vegetables for this recipe, but you can eat them on their own! Just remove the bay leaves beforehand).

TOFU CHORIZO

2 tbsp.	chipotle purée (Embasa brand)	4 cloves	garlic, minced
4 cloves	garlic	½ tsp.	ground cinnamon
1 tbsp.	dry oregano	2 tbsp.	apple cider vinegar
2 tsp.	paprika	3 tbsp.	organic peanut butter
1 ½ tsp.	cumin	½ recipe	Vegetable Stock (save and freeze the rest!)
1 tsp.	sea salt		
⅛ tsp.	red pepper flakes	1 pound	silken tofu, firm and drained

1. Place all ingredients, except for the tofu, into a pan and whisk together over medium-high heat until incorporated.
2. Crumble the tofu into the saucepan and turn the heat down to medium-low.
3. Cook until dry and crumbly, about 15 to 20 minutes, stirring frequently.

BLACK BEAN PURÉE

2 cans	cooked black beans	1 clove	garlic
¼ cup	water	½ tsp.	sea salt

Place everything in a blender and blend until smooth.

CHIPOTLE HOLLANDAISE

3 tbsp.	vegan butter	1 tbsp.	vegan mayo
2 tbsp.	unbleached organic flour	1 tbsp.	chipotle purée
1 pinch	turmeric	1 half	lemon, juiced
1 cup	unsweetened soy milk	½ tsp.	sea salt
2 tbsp.	nutritional yeast	⅛ tsp.	ground black pepper

1. Heat the butter in a small saucepan until melted. Whisk in the flour to make a roux.
2. Add the pinch of turmeric. (This is for color.)
3. Slowly whisk in the soy milk, then bring the sauce to a boil until thickened.
4. Boil for 2 minutes and remove from the heat.
5. Whisk in the nutritional yeast, vegan mayo, chipotle purée, lemon juice, salt and pepper.

ASSEMBLY

3 tbsp.	vegan butter	12 slices	heirloom tomatoes
6 whole	vegan English muffins, cut in half	1 ½ cups	Tofu Chorizo
1 ½ cups	Black Bean Purée	1 ½ cups	Chipotle Hollandaise

1. Preheat the oven to 350°F. Spread the butter over each muffin half.
2. Place the muffin on a baking sheet and bake for 8 to 10 minutes or until golden brown. Remove from the oven and set on a plate.
3. Place the Black Bean Purée in a sauté pan and heat on medium-low for 3 to 4 minutes.
4. Spread ¼ cup of hot Black Bean Purée on each piece of muffin.
5. Top with a slice of heirloom tomato.
6. Place ¼ cup of hot Tofu Chorizo on top of the tomato and smother with the Chipotle Hollandaise.

SPICY BLOODY HARRY

There's a lot to be said for reading the fine print. If you do, you'll find that a Bloody Mary vegetable elixir isn't actually vegan, thanks to those anchovies swimming around the Worcestershire sauce. Sound fishy? We thought so. Thus, we introduce Bloody Harry-Mary's fishless cousin.

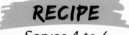
RECIPE
Serves 4 to 6

ANCHO CHILI PASTE

1.5 ounce package	dried whole chilies

1. In a pot, add 6 cups of water and ancho chilies in a pot and bring to a boil.
2. Then reduce to medium heat and cook for about 10 minutes. Remove from heat and let cool.
3. Strain the mixture, saving the liquid.
4. Rinse chilies under cold water to remove all seeds and stem. Place the chilies in a blender with 2 cups of the strained liquid and blend until smooth.

BLOODY HARRY

2 cups	Ancho Chili Paste	2 tbsp.	hot sauce
2 cups	tomato juice	1 tbsp.	green olive liquid
2 cups	8 vegetable juice blend	½ tsp.	ground black pepper
½ cup	orange juice	1 tsp.	sea salt
½ cup	lime juice	8 fluid oz	vodka or tequila
½ cup	vegan Worcestershire sauce		

GARNISH

6 small	pickled pearl onions	6 slices	Native Bacon (page 23)
6 whole	cornichons	6 sticks	celery
6 whole	green olives		

1. Add the paste and the rest of the Bloody Harry ingredients to the blender and blend until smooth. You may need to do this in separate batches.
2. Grab a pint glass, fill with ice then pour in 2 ounces of vodka or tequila each, and 1 cup of the Bloody Harry mix. Garnish with skewered pickled onions, cornichon and green olives, along with a bacon stirrer and celery stick.

TWICE-BAKED SAVORY BREAKFAST CAKES

Finish these pseudo eggs off any way you want—'veg' sour cream, green onions, crispy shallots or non-dairy cheddar. It's up to you, chef. Basically, we're saying this dish is downright good, no matter how you whisk it.

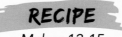

RECIPE

Makes 12-15

POLENTA CAKES

3 cups	broccoli, steamed and finely chopped	2 tsp.	sea salt
		3 tbsp.	vegan butter
6 cups	water	1 cup	vegan cheddar cheese, shredded
1 ¾ cups	polenta		

1. Bring 6 cups of water to a boil in a large saucepot.
2. Gradually whisk in the polenta. Reduce the heat to low and cook until the mixture thickens and polenta is tender, stirring often, about 10 to 12 minutes.
3. Turn off the heat. Add salt, butter and cheese. Stir until melted.
4. Add in broccoli and stir mixture. Cool by laying mixture flat on a baking sheet in the refrigerator until ready to cut.
5. Using a round cutter, (3 ¼ inch in size), punch out the polenta cakes.

NATIVE BACON

3 tbsp.	vegetable oil	1 to 2 drops	liquid smoke (optional)
1 block	silken tofu, extra-firm	3 tbsp.	nutritional yeast
3 tbsp.	soy sauce or tamari		

1. Preheat oil in a fry pan on medium heat.
2. Slice the tofu into thin strips (like bacon) and add to fry pan, turning once until crispy on each side.
3. Add soy sauce and 1 to 2 drops of liquid smoke (to taste, one drop at a time). Toss with the bacon slices, sprinkle with the nutritional yeast and remove from heat.

ASSEMBLY

1 recipe	Polenta Cakes		1 recipe	Native Bacon
2 tbsp.	safflower oil or vegetable oil			

1. Using a sauté pan, heat oil. Place 4 to 6 Polenta Cakes in the hot oil and sauté for 2 minutes or until golden brown. Flip and repeat on the other side.
2. Lay bacon pieces over warm Polenta Cakes.
3. Top with your choice of chives, shallots, salsa, green onions and more!

OH MAMA! ITALIAN BREAKFAST PIZZA

Fight the late-night leftover pizza craving and save it for the morning, when you can whip up a homemade breakfast pizza complete with tofu scramble, kale and vegan sausage. Lay out some extra fixings for the family and indulge to your stomach's delight.

RECIPE
Makes 3, 10-inch pizzas

NATIVE SCRAMBLE

6 tbsp.	olive oil	½ tsp.	sea salt
1 ½ cups	onion, chopped	¼ tsp.	black pepper
¾ cup	red bell peppers, chopped	½ tsp.	turmeric
3 pounds	silken tofu, medium or firm, crumbled	¾ cup	green bell peppers, chopped

1. Heat olive oil in a sauté pan. Add the onions and the bell pepper and sauté for 1 to 2 minutes until translucent.
2. Lower the heat and add the crumbled tofu. Using a rubber spatula, scramble all ingredients together. Allow to cook for 2 to 3 minutes.
3. Add salt, pepper and turmeric. Adjust seasoning if necessary.

If you're only baking for one or two, wrap the leftover, uncooked dough balls in plastic wrap and store in the freezer. Simply defrost at room temperature (or overnight in the refrigerator) for the next time you're hungry.

BASIL PESTO
Makes 2 cups

6 cloves	garlic	3 cups	basil leaves, lightly packed
½ cup	pine nuts, toasted	⅛ tsp.	ground black pepper
½ cup	walnuts	¼ tsp.	lemon juice
½ cup	pumpkin seeds, toasted	½ tsp.	sea salt
1 ½ cups	olive oil		

1. Purée garlic, pine nuts, walnuts and pumpkin seeds in a food processor with olive oil.
2. Add remaining ingredients and blend.

PIZZA DOUGH

1 cup	water, warm	3 cups	unbleached organic flour
2 ½ tsp.	active dry yeast	1 tbsp.	olive oil
1 tbsp.	granulated sugar	¼ cup	Kalamata olives, pits removed and chopped

1. In a mixer, add the water and yeast and mix for about 2 to 3 minutes.
2. Add the rest of the ingredients and mix for another 3 to 4 minutes on medium speed until mixed.
3. Remove dough and place it on a lightly floured pan (so it doesn't stick).
4. Cut the dough in 3 pieces and roll each into a ball.
5. Place onto a sheet pan with a little bit of oil on the bottom, brushing a little more oil on the top. Cover with plastic wrap and place dough near the stove for 20 minutes.
6. Remove from sheet pan and, one at a time, place on the counter with a little bit of flour covering your surface and lightly dusted on the dough.
7. Press the dough with fingertips to release the air and begin to stretch the dough until it's about 10 inches in size.
8. Place on a dry sheet pan and bake at 350°F for about 2 to 3 minutes.
9. Remove from heat and let cool.

ASSEMBLY
Makes 1 pizza

1 whole	tomato, chopped	⅓ recipe	pizza dough
2 leaves	basil, chiffonade	⅓ recipe	Native Scramble
1 clove	garlic, minced	2 cups	vegan sausage, crumbled (try Upton's Naturals Italian Seitan)
1 to 2 tbsp.	olive oil		
¼ tsp.	sea salt	1 cup	kale, steamed and chopped
1 pinch	black pepper	¼ cup	Basil Pesto
¼ cup	marinara	¼ cup	vegan mozzarella (optional)

1. In a small bowl, mix chopped tomato with basil leaf, garlic, oil, salt and pepper.
2. Spread marinara all over crust leaving ¼-inch border around the edges.
3. Top marinara in the following order: Native Scramble, vegan sausage, kale, tomato-basil mixture and vegan mozzarella.
4. Bake at 400°F in the oven for 10 minutes.
5. Drizzle Basil Pesto over top in a zigzag fashion.

BLUEBERRY THRILL COBBLER

We owe this delicacy to the British American colonists who once lacked the ingredients to make typical pies. Instead, they placed sweet fruit in pans, filled in the holes with a thick batter and topped them off with a layer of warm, crispy biscuits. Ours looks similar, and it's just as unique.

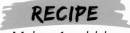

RECIPE

Makes 1 cobbler

BLUEBERRY FILLING

4 cups	fresh blueberries	¾ cup	organic sugar
1 tsp.	vanilla extract	½ tsp.	unbleached organic flour
1 half	lemon, juiced	1 tbsp.	vegan butter, melted

1. Lightly grease an 8 x 8-inch baking dish. Place the blueberries in a bowl and add vanilla and lemon juice.
2. Add sugar and flour, then stir in the tablespoon of melted butter. Pour into the baking dish and set aside.

COBBLER BATTER

1 ¾ cups	unbleached organic flour	5 tbsp.	vegan butter, cold
4 tsp.	baking powder	1 cup	almond or coconut milk
5 tbsp.	organic sugar		

We recommend a bit of non-dairy coconut
vanilla bean ice cream on the side.

29

1. In a medium bowl, stir together flour, baking powder and sugar. Cut the cold butter into small pieces, then rub into mixture well until in small pieces.
2. Make a well in the center and quickly stir in the milk. Mix just until moistened. You should have a very thick batter or very wet dough. If you need to, add a splash of non-dairy milk.
3. Cover and let batter rest for 10 minutes.

ASSEMBLY

1 recipe	Cobbler Batter	1 pinch	cinnamon
1 recipe	Blueberry Filling	2 tsp.	organic sugar

1. Preheat the oven to 375°F. Spoon the batter over the blueberries, leaving only a few small holes for the berries to peek through. Mix together the cinnamon and 2 teaspoons of sugar and sprinkle over top.
2. Bake 20 to 25 minutes or until golden brown. Let cool until just warm before serving.

DITCH DAY

- Vegetable "Pot Pie" with Fresh Thyme Biscuits & Maple Butter
- The Delish Knish
- Homestyle Seitan Meatloaf
- Weird Al's Tamale Pie
- Chili Verde Vegan
- Boston Crème Pie

It's true. There's an actual day to celebrate ditching your New Year's resolutions. And if you're already anxious about getting there, it's January 17th to be exact. We'd say that's a pretty pathetic date—a whole two weeks of resolving. But don't worry—these plant-based recipes can help you indulge without the guilt.

These next one-pot dishes are what you might call "comfort foods" for their flaky, buttery crusts and hearty fillings. They're easy to make and even easier to share, so whip them up for family and friends and treat yourself to just a serving (or two).

VEGETABLE "POT PIE" WITH FRESH THYME BISCUITS & MAPLE BUTTER

*T*his heavenly combo has us weak in the knees. Heart-warming and rich—it sounds like our kind of guy. Sorry, pie! Say no more, we're already in love.

RECIPE
Serves 2

THYME BISCUITS
Makes 6 biscuits

1 tbsp.	baking powder	4 tbsp.	butter, cold and cut in tiny pieces
½ tsp.	sea salt	¾ cup	rice milk
2 cups	unbleached organic flour	¼ cup	fresh thyme, chopped

1. Mix the baking powder, salt and flour together. Mix on low speed for 1 ½ minutes using the paddle attachment.
2. Add 2 tablespoons of cold butter at a time, still on low.
3. Add the rice milk and thyme and mix well.
4. Preheat oven to 450°F.
5. On a wax-lined baking sheet, drop ¼ cup of batter into biscuits, 3 inches from each other.
6. Bake at 450°F for 10 to 12 minutes.

MAPLE BUTTER

½ cup	vegan butter	1 tbsp.	maple syrup

1. Allow the butter to soften at room temperature, about 20 minutes.
2. Place the butter and maple syrup in a bowl and mix well with a whisk until the syrup is incorporated.
3. Allow the butter to cool for at least 1 hour to firm up before serving.

STEW

½ cup	water	½ tsp.	ground black pepper
2 cloves	garlic, minced	1 tsp.	garlic powder
¾ cup	onions, diced	3 cups	non-dairy milk
⅔ cup	carrots, diced	⅓ cup	red peppers, diced
⅓ cup	potatoes, diced	2 tbsp.	fresh thyme, chopped
¼ cup	vegan butter, melted	2 tbsp.	parsley, chopped
¾ cup	unbleached organic flour	½ cup	peas
1 tsp.	sea salt		

1. Place ½ cup of water in a medium-sized pan. On medium-high heat, add the garlic and onions. Cook for 2 minutes.
2. Add the carrots and potatoes and cook 2 more minutes.
3. Add the butter to the veggies and coat with flour (making a roux).
4. Add the salt, pepper and garlic powder.
5. Whisk in the milk. Make sure no lumps form.
6. Add the red peppers.
7. Allow the pot to come to a slow boil. This will thicken the mix.
8. Then turn the mix down and add the fresh herbs and peas.
9. Simmer for 10 minutes or until the potatoes are fork-tender. You may add water if the mix begins to get too thick.
10. Serve in a nice round bowl and enjoy with Thyme Biscuits and Maple Butter.

THE DELISH KNISH

While most of us know the Italian calzone, the Spanish empanada, and the Polish pierogi, not all are familiar with the "Yiddish knish" (try that one five times fast). We love ours with mashed potatoes, tofu and onions, especially on a lazy day with the family.

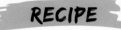

RECIPE

Makes 24 little or 16 big knishes

DOUGH

2 quarts	water	1 tsp.	sea salt
1 cup	russet potatoes	1 tsp.	baking soda
3 cups	unbleached organic flour (or pastry flour)	1 tbsp.	safflower oil
		1 cup	water, cold

1. Place 2 quarts of water in a large pot and bring to a boil. Peel potatoes and cut into quarters. Boil them until they are fork tender, about 20 minutes.
2. Strain the potatoes and mash them with a fork or masher.
3. In a bowl, sift the flour, salt and baking soda together.
4. Add the mash potatoes and mix. Add the oil and water and mix until the dough is formed. (You can do this by hand or in a mixer). Set aside.

KNISH FILLING

2 tbsp.	safflower oil	1 tsp.	garlic powder
1 cup	yellow onion, diced	1 ½ cups	russet potatoes, mashed
1 tsp.	sea salt	14 oz	silken tofu, firm and mashed
½ tsp.	ground black pepper		

1. Heat the oil in a sauté pan and add the onions. Cook for 1 minute.
2. Add the salt, black pepper and garlic powder and cook for 2 more minutes, or until translucent.
3. Place the mashed potato and tofu in a food processor and blend until smooth.
4. Fold in the sautéed onions.

ASSEMBLY

1. Preheat oven to 350°F and grease a baking sheet or line it with parchment paper.
2. Using your hands, take a golf ball-sized piece of dough, rolling and flattening into a disc shape.
3. Continuously roll in your hands, and begin to form a basket in the middle of the dough in your palm. Place about 1 tablespoon of filling in the basket.
4. Fold over and pinch every end of the dough to lock the filling inside. The dough will bind together easily.
5. Place the knish fold side down on a baking sheet. Repeat until all the dough is formed.
6. Bake for 25 minutes and allow to cool for 5 minutes before eating.

HOMESTYLE SEITAN MEATLOAF

We're convinced this veg-loaf is better than the original (and healthier too). Meatier recipes may take a backseat after this vegan version storms the kitchen.

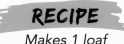

RECIPE
Makes 1 loaf

4 cups	seitan, ground	⅓ cup	organic ketchup
1 medium	sweet onion, quartered	2 tbsp.	soy sauce
1 medium	carrot, chopped	½ cup	tomato sauce
2 cloves	garlic, pressed	to taste	sea salt and pepper
1 cup	breadcrumbs	to taste	fresh parsley and thyme
⅓ cup	almond or peanut butter		

1. Place the ground seitan in a large bowl.
2. Place the quartered onion, carrot and garlic in a food processor and process for 15 to 20 seconds. Veggies should be diced small, not puréed.
3. Preheat your oven to 375°F and lightly grease a loaf pan.
4. Add the ground up veggies and all other ingredients to the bowl of ground seitan. Mix well. Taste and adjust seasonings if needed.
5. Place in loaf pan and bake for 40 to 50 minutes.

WEIRD AL'S TAMALE PIE

Weird Al Yankovic is many things—parodist, musician, author, total quirk-ster…and a Native Foods friend. So we asked for his family recipe box—figuring his favorites were anything but traditional—and found his grandmother's Tamale Pie. We loved the vibrant flavors so much we *had* to do it up vegan style. We dare you to get a little weird and try this pie out.

RECIPE

Makes 16 pieces

TAMALE FILLING

½ cup	olive oil	2 cups	tomatoes, chopped
2 cups	red onion, diced into ¼-inch	2 cups	sweet corn kernels, drained
5 cloves	garlic, peeled and chopped	2 tbsp.	chipotle canned chiles, chopped
2 cups	red pepper, diced into ¼-inch	2 tsp.	cumin
2 tsp.	sea salt	2 tbsp.	coriander spice
3 cups	canned kidney beans, strained for 10 minutes		

1. Preheat oven to 325°F.
2. Heat olive oil in skillet and sauté onions, garlic, red peppers and salt until lightly browned.
3. Add kidney beans, tomatoes, corn, chopped chipotle, cumin and coriander and simmer for 10 minutes. Make sure to strain the beans, corn and tomatoes for 10 minutes before using.
4. Spread mixture evenly into a 9 x 13-inch pan.

CORNBREAD MIXTURE

1 ½ cups	unbleached organic flour	½ cup	safflower oil
1 ¼ cups	corn flour	7 ounces	silken tofu, firm
1 tbsp.	baking soda	½ cup	agave nectar
1 tbsp.	baking powder	2 ¼ cups	orange juice
½ tbsp.	sea salt	1 half	orange, zested
½ cup	water		

1. Sift all dry ingredients together in a mixing bowl.
2. In a blender, place the water, oil, tofu and agave and blend until smooth.
3. Slowly add the wet ingredients into the mixing bowl and fold in. Add in the orange juice and orange zest. Continue to fold and mix.

ASSEMBLY

1 recipe	Cornbread Mixture	1 recipe	Tamale Filling

1. Pour Cornbread Mixture over Tamale Filling and spread with a spatula.
2. Bake in oven at 325°F for about 35 to 40 minutes. Check often and rotate pan while baking.
3. Remove from oven. Let cool and refrigerate until ready to cut.

CHILI VERDE VEGAN

*T*his one-pot-wonder can be served over rice or avocado slices for a hefty meal. It's an easy one to make, too—just throw these aromatic ingredients together over the stove and let the flavors infuse on their own.

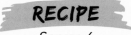
RECIPE
Serves 6

SEITAN BROTH

12 cups	water	10 whole	black peppercorns
1 ½ cups	low-sodium soy sauce	4 whole	bay leaves
6 cloves	garlic	2 pieces	Kombu, 2 x ½-inch in size
2 pieces	ginger, sliced into 1 inch		

1. Place all ingredients into a large stockpot and bring to a rapid boil. Reduce to a simmer for the seitan cooking (boiling soy sauce will make it saltier).
2. Make sure to save the broth after using, you can freeze it and reuse it to make this recipe again!

ORIGINAL SEITAN
Makes 2 pounds or 2 loaves

2 cups	vital wheat flour	½ cup	low-sodium soy sauce
6 tbsp.	nutritional yeast flakes	2 tbsp.	olive oil
2 tsp.	onion powder	4 tbsp.	lemon juice
2 tsp.	ground black pepper	4 cloves	garlic, minced
1 cup	water or Vegetable Stock (page 17)	for assembly	cheesecloth and twine

Kombu is an eatable kelp that aids in digestion. Not only does it prevent gaseousness, it also adds a good supply of iodine and fiber.

1. Combine the vital wheat flour, yeast flakes, onion powder and pepper in a bowl. Mix well.
2. In a separate bowl, combine the water or stock, soy sauce, oil, lemon juice and garlic.
3. Slowly add the liquid to the flour bowl. Using your hands or a wooden spoon, mix until most of the moisture is combined. Some dry bits are fine.
4. Remove the dough from the bowl and place on a cutting board or clean surface. Knead for 3 to 4 minutes.
5. Divide the dough into 2 loaves (about 1 pound each).
6. Tightly wrap each loaf with cheesecloth and tie off the string on both ends using twine.
7. Once the broth has boiled, bring it down to a low simmer. Place the loaves in the pot and cover halfway with a lid. Allow the steam to be released. (Never boil while cooking seitan.)
8. Simmer for 45 minutes. Then turn the heat off and allow the loaves to sit in the pot for 15 to 20 more minutes.
9. Remove the cheesecloth while still warm. If you don't, it will stick!

LIME CILANTRO CREAM

1 cup	vegan sour cream	1 tbsp.	lime juice
2 tbsp.	cilantro, chopped	½ tsp.	smoked paprika
1 whole	lime, zested		

Place all ingredients in a bowl and whisk together.

CHILI VERDE

¼ cup	olive oil	½ pound	tomatillos
2 whole	onions, chopped into ¼-inch pieces	½ bunch	cilantro, washed, stems removed and chopped
1 tbsp.	sea salt	2 tsp.	dry oregano
1 medium	red bell pepper, chopped into ¼-inch pieces	1 tsp.	cumin
		1 tsp.	coriander
1 recipe	Original Seitan, cut into 1-inch pieces	1 whole	bay leaf
		2 cups	Vegetable Stock (page 17)
¼ cup	unbleached organic flour	2 to 3 tsp.	vegan adobo sauce
4 cloves	garlic, diced	½ tsp.	ground black pepper
2 whole	Anaheim chilies	12 whole	corn tortillas, warmed

1. Roast Anaheim chilies. (See Roasted Pepper recipe on page 291 and cut roasting time in half. Peel chilies and chop into ½-inch pieces after roasting.)
2. Remove husks and broil tomatillos until charred. Purée in blender.
3. Heat olive oil in stockpot and sauté onion, salt and red pepper until onion is transparent and lightly browned. Then add seitan and stir for one minute.
4. Add flour and stir for another minute.
5. Add the rest of the ingredients, stir well and simmer for 40 minutes.
6. Put tortillas on a baking pan. Heat for 2 to 3 minutes, and serve with the chili and Lime Cilantro Cream.

BOSTON CRÈME PIE

This "pie" (psst, it's actually a cake) is la crème de la crème of American desserts. And after we whipped up our vegan version, it became the custard cream of our crop, too.

RECIPE
Serves 8

VANILLA CAKE

1 ¼ cups	unbleached organic flour	¼ cup	vegetable oil
¼ cup	organic sugar	1 ½ tsp.	apple cider vinegar
1 tsp.	baking powder	¾ cup	rice milk
¼ tsp.	baking soda	1 tsp.	vanilla extract
¼ tsp.	sea salt		

1. Preheat oven to 375°F.
2. Combine flour, sugar, baking powder, baking soda and salt in a bowl. Mix well.
3. In a separate bowl, mix vegetable oil with apple cider vinegar and let sit for a few minutes, then mix in rice milk and vanilla.
4. Pour the liquid ingredients into the dry while mixing in.
5. Place cake mixture into a 10-inch pie tin and bake for 20 to 25 minutes.
6. Remove and let cool completely.
7. Cut top off cooled cake. Save both halves.

BOSTON CRÈME

14 ounces	silken tofu, firm	2 tbsp.	coconut oil
1 cup	powdered sugar	⅛ tsp.	turmeric
1 tbsp.	vanilla extract		

1. Put the silken tofu, powdered sugar and vanilla in food processor.
2. Melt the coconut oil with the turmeric over low heat, then put into food processor with the tofu mixture and purée until smooth.

ASSEMBLY

1 recipe	Boston Crème	2 tbsp.	vegan butter
1 recipe	Vanilla Cake	½ cup	rice milk
1 cup	vegan chocolate chips		

1. Pour the crème over top of cake in pan and put cake top back on upside down, so that cut part is facing up.
2. Place chocolate chips, butter and milk in a double boiler.
3. Place 1 to 2 inches of water in saucepan and bring to boil with chocolate in bowl on top to cover.
4. Let chips melt, mix well and pour over the cake.
5. Refrigerate well before serving.

TOUCHDOWN!

- Warm Spinach Artichoke Dip
- Wild Card Wings with Spicy Apricot BBQ Sauce
- Chili Lime Yam Chips
- Extra Point 8-Layer Dip
- Miyamoto Japanese Nachos
- Chocolate Peanut Butter Bars
- Swedish Wheat Balls

Super Bowl Sunday is quite possibly the most American celebration (shhh…don't tell the Fourth of July). It's a beloved tradition that runs through American blood and spirit—it's pretty much "Native" to the U. S. of A. And while around 48 million Americans will choose to order in for their family and guests, make your celebration special with home-made, touchdown-worthy traditions.

Like dip. Did you know that one third of people eat some version of dip on Super Bowl Sunday? And that it's the second highest day of food consumption after Thanksgiving? That said, it can be hard to go healthy, let alone go vegan today. But get this—veggies top the list of foods eaten at home during the big game. Now there's something to cheer about!

These indulgent recipes are just what you'll want by your side during nail-biters on the gridiron, controversial play reviews and those loveable commercials. From our "wings" to nachos to yes, of course, the dips, your guests will be begging for this all-American recipe playbook.

WARM SPINACH ARTICHOKE DIP

This dip can be served cold with pita and veggies, or hot as a casserole with vegan cheese on top. Either way you go, one of them will be a winner.

RECIPE
Serves 8

3 cups	canned artichoke hearts, water-packed	½ cup	vegan cream cheese
		1 tsp.	sea salt
1 lb. bag	frozen spinach	6 tbsp.	nutritional yeast
1 cup	vegan sour cream	½ tsp.	garlic powder
½ cup	vegan mayo		

1. Drain water from artichoke hearts.
2. Place all ingredients in a bowl or mixing container.
3. Using a hand blender, mix until incorporated and a smooth and creamy texture is achieved, scraping sides as needed.
4. Place the dip in oven-safe serving bowl and bake at 350°F for 12 to 15 minutes or until golden and bubbly on top.
5. Serve with veggie crudité, crostini, baguette or tortilla chips.

WILD CARD WINGS WITH SPICY APRICOT BBQ SAUCE

You can easily start your own "chicken" wing tradition with the help of a little seitan and spicy sauce. This recipe will have you back in the game, vegan-style.

RECIPE
Makes 18 to 22 pieces

SPICY APRICOT BBQ SAUCE
Makes 1 ½ cups

1 pound	apricots, fresh, pits removed and halved	1 whole	yellow onion, diced
3 medium	tomatoes, quartered	4 cloves	garlic, minced
2 cups	organic brown sugar	2 tbsp.	soy sauce
¼ cup	molasses	¼ cup	hot sauce (choose your heat)
1 tsp.	liquid smoke	2 tsp.	Dijon mustard
2 cups	apple cider vinegar	1 tsp.	celery salt

1. Place all ingredients into a saucepan and bring to a boil.
2. Reduce the heat and simmer for 1 to 1 ½ hours, add water if needed. Remove from heat, pour into a bowl.
3. Using a hand blender, blend until smooth.

WINGS

½ cup	unbleached organic flour	1 pound	Original Seitan (page 41), cut into 1 x ½-inch strips
¼ cup	garlic powder		
¼ cup	onion powder	1 cup	water
		for frying	safflower or grape seed oil

1. Place the flour and spices into a bowl and mix well.
2. Dip the seitan pieces in the water bowl then toss in the flour. Coat well.
3. Heat the oil in a sauté pan until hot. A good test is to sprinkle flour in it. If the flour begins to sizzle, the pan is ready.
4. Place the wings into the hot oil carefully, and allow each side to get golden and crispy, about 2 minutes per side.
5. Remove from the pan and allow them to dry on a paper towel to remove the excess oil. Enjoy with Spicy Apricot BBQ Sauce.

CHILI LIME YAM CHIPS

With so many dips going around, you need the perfect scooper to take them down. These yam chips are just as crunchy as tortilla chips and can be used next to whatever you're serving. Careful, you could end up just eating these tasty chips solo.

RECIPE

Makes 12 cups

| 16 to 18 ounces | yams | 2 tbsp. | chile con limon |
| 1 quart | vegetable oil | | |

1. Peel and cut whole yam in half widthwise and place side by side in food processor. Using the smallest blade, slice at medium speed. You may also use a mandolin.
2. Rinse with cold water, drain. Dry thoroughly.
3. Drop chips into a 350°F pot of vegetable oil. Using a slotted spoon, stir chips so they don't stick. Remove from the pan when golden brown. Place on paper towels to remove excess oil.
4. Place in a bowl and toss with chile con limon spice using tongs.

EXTRA POINT 8-LAYER DIP

Got a room to feed? This piled-high and deeply satisfying dip will have your guests tackling each other for more. Just make sure to have napkins on hand—it's not our neatest creation.

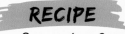

RECIPE

Serves 6 to 8

SPICY BEANS

2 tbsp.	safflower oil	1 to 2 whole	jalapeño, veins and seeds removed
5 cloves	garlic, minced		
1 cup	yellow onion, diced	2 cups	organic kidney beans, cooked or canned (drained)

1. Heat the oil, garlic, onion and jalapeño in a saucepan until translucent and aromatic. Add the cooked kidney beans and cook for 2 to 3 more minutes.
2. Using the back of a spoon, roughly mash the mix. You may add a bit of bean liquid or water to do this. Or place in a blender and blend until smooth. Set aside and allow to cool.

TACO MEAT

1 pound	Mexican Seitan (½ Original Seitan recipe on page 41, with 1 tablespoon ground paprika, 2 teaspoons cumin, 2 teaspoons cayenne pepper and 1 tablespoon dried oregano)	2 tbsp.	safflower oil
		3 cloves	garlic, minced
		½ cup	yellow onion, diced

1. When the loaf is cooled, cut it into pieces small enough to be placed into a food processor. Then grind until crumbly.
2. Heat the oil, garlic and onions in a pan until translucent. Add the ground seitan and mix well. Allow to cool.

GUACAMOLE

2 whole	avocados, peeled and pitted		1 tsp.	cumin
¼ cup	red onions, diced		¼ cup	cilantro, chopped
1 tbsp.	lime juice		1 clove	garlic, minced
1 tsp.	sea salt			

Place the avocados, red onions, lime juice, salt and cumin in a bowl. Using a fork, mash until you get a "rustic" looking guacamole. Fold in the chopped cilantro and minced garlic.

ASSEMBLY

1 cup	vegan sour cream		½ cup	scallions, sliced
2 whole	tomatoes, diced		1 recipe	Spicy Beans
1 cup	vegan cheddar cheese, shredded		1 recipe	Taco Meat
1 cup	black olives, sliced and pitted		1 recipe	Guacamole

1. Using a glass serving dish, pie shell or bowl, layer the ingredients in any order you want.
2. Serve with tortilla chips or a big giant spoon!

MIYAMOTO JAPANESE NACHOS

Nachos have been around the world and back, and in this recipe they've packed wasabi, ginger and seaweed into their carry-ons.

RECIPE
Serves 6

YAM CHIPS

1 pound	yams, peeled	½ tsp.	sea salt
¼ cup	olive oil		

1. Preheat oven to 425°F.
2. Slice yams into ⅛-inch slices. Place in bowl and rinse with cold water. Drain.
3. Toss yams with olive oil in bowl.
4. Line two baking pans with parchment paper and lay the yam slices down in a single layer. Sprinkle sea salt on top.
5. Bake for 10 minutes, then turn and bake for another 10.

TOMATO MIX

4 whole	Roma tomatoes, diced	2 whole	green onions, finely chopped
1 half	cucumber, peeled, seeded and sliced in ¼-inch pieces	½ tsp.	sea salt
½ tsp.	fresh ginger, minced	1 tbsp.	toasted sesame seeds (mix of black and white look great)

While yams are baking, toss tomato, cucumber, ginger, green onion, salt and toasted sesame seeds together.

WASABI AIOLI

2 tsp.	wasabi powder		2 tsp.	lemon juice
2 tbsp.	water		½ tsp.	soy sauce
¾ cup	vegan mayo		½ tsp.	maple syrup

1. Mix wasabi powder with water to form a paste. Be careful of the fumes.
2. In a small bowl, whisk together the mayo, lemon juice, soy sauce and maple syrup and then add the wasabi paste.

ASSEMBLY

2 cups	black beans		1 whole	avocado, chopped in ½-inch cubes
1 recipe	Yam Chips		1 recipe	Wasabi Aioli
1 recipe	Tomato Mix		½ cup	nori strips

1. Warm beans on stovetop.
2. Arrange Yam Chips on platter and top with black beans, Tomato Mix and avocado.
3. Drizzle the Wasabi Aioli over the top in a zigzag fashion and garnish with nori strips.

CHOCOLATE PEANUT BUTTER CUPS

These heavenly PB and…C desserts are so good you might find yourself sneaking off with them during the halftime show.

RECIPE

Makes 12 peanut butter cups

CRUST

1 cup	unbleached organic flour	4 tbsp.	vegan butter
4 tbsp.	organic sugar	4 tbsp.	safflower oil
⅛ tsp.	sea salt	½ cup	peanuts, roughly chopped

1. Mix all ingredients together in a small bowl.
2. Line a cupcake tin with cupcake liners and evenly distribute the mix and push down.
3. Bake at 350°F for 8 to 10 minutes. Then allow them to cool completely before filling.

FILLING

1 ⅓ cups	vegan peanut butter	1 cup	powdered sugar
1 cup	vegan butter	½ cup	water

1. Mix together the peanut butter and butter until creamy.
2. Add in the powdered sugar and mix well.
3. Mix in the water.
4. Place ⅓ cup of sweet peanut butter mix into each chilled, crusted cupcake liner.
5. Allow the cups to chill for 3 to 4 hours to firm up.

CHOCOLATE TOPPING

2 ¾ cups	vegan chocolate chips	¼ cup	soy milk

1. Place the chocolate chips and soy milk in the top of a double boiler over water.
2. Allow the chips to melt slowly and whisk occasionally. Do not overcook or heat the chips too quickly. They will begin to "curdle" up and get chunky, not smooth.
3. Once the chocolate is smooth and creamy, evenly pour the chocolate on top of the 12 peanut butter cups. Place the cups back in the fridge until firm. This may take a few hours. Overnight will get the best firmness.

SWEDISH WHEAT BALLS

Sure, they look more like Ping-Pong balls than footballs, but that's so they'll pop perfectly in your mouth for a bite-sized winner.

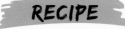

RECIPE

Makes 3 dozen balls

WHEAT BALLS

1 pound	Swedish Seitan (½ Original Seitan recipe on page 41, adding ½ tsp. of ground nutmeg, allspice, and cloves, as well as 1 tsp. ground black pepper in first step of recipe)	¾ cup	soy milk (with 1 tsp. of apple cider vinegar)
		2 tbsp.	safflower oil
		3 cloves	garlic, minced
		1 cup	yellow onion, diced
¾ cup	breadcrumbs	¼ cup	water
		4 tbsp.	wheat gluten

1. Preheat the oven to 350°F.
2. Cut the seitan loaf into small pieces. Place in the food processor and grind. Put into a large mixing bowl and set aside.
3. Place the breadcrumbs and soy milk in another bowl and allow it to sit for 10 to 15 minutes, or until soft.
4. Heat the oil in a sauté pan and add the garlic and onions. Cook until translucent and add to the ground seitan bowl.
5. Add the soft breadcrumbs, water and wheat gluten to the seitan bowl and mix well.
6. Form the mix into small (about 2 tablespoons each) meatballs. If they don't stick together, add more wheat gluten and try again.
7. Place the seitan balls on a baking sheet lined with parchment paper.
8. Bake for 20 to 25 minutes. Flip halfway for even browning.

CREAMY DILL SAUCE

¼ cup	vegan butter	½ tsp.	sea salt
¼ cup	unbleached organic flour	¼ cup	fresh dill, chopped
2 cups	soy milk		

1. Melt the butter in a saucepan. Whisk in the flour to make a blonde roux and cook for 1 minute.
2. Slowly whisk the soy milk in. Continue whisking to eliminate lumps that may form.
3. Allow the sauce to come to a boil, slowly, in order for it to thicken.
4. Once the sauce is thick, remove the pan from the heat and add the salt and chopped dill.
5. Serve over the Swedish Wheat Balls or on the side.

LOVE BITES

- Il Dolce! Tiramisu
- Garlic Bread
- Truffle Asparagus Risotto
- Caesar Salad
- Heart Beet Soup
- Native Lasagna
- Cardamom Rose Cupcakes

We like to do Valentine's Day the mushy romantic way, not necessarily the historic way. The origins of Valentine's Day all date back to Rome around the third century, when the empire almost collapsed. There certainly wasn't much love going around, to say the least. But as lovers and peacekeepers ourselves, we thought we'd do Valentine's Day the modern way, with heart-warming menus.

Cook for him, cook for her, cook together, you pick! But make an evening out of it with the homey touch of candles, oven smells, and intimate moments. Leave it up to these Native recipes to propel your amorous vibes and to be your Cupid for the night.

IL DOLCE! TIRAMISU

*O*h tiramisu, how we love you so. Do us a favor and be our Valentine, no? Tiramisu, which literally means "pick me up," referring to the coffee liqueur, is sure to put you and yours in good spirits.

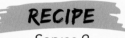

RECIPE
Serves 9

LADYFINGERS

2 cups	unbleached organic flour	1 cup	safflower oil
1 ¼ cups	organic sugar	½ cup	water
3 tsp.	baking powder	¾ cup	rice milk
2 tsp.	organic corn starch	½ tsp.	almond extract
1 tsp.	vanilla extract		

1. Preheat oven to 350°F.
2. Grease a 9 x 13-inch pan, then dust with flour.
3. Place all dry ingredients together in a mixer and sift on medium for 1 minute.
4. Lower the speed and slowly add the wet ingredients to the dry.
5. Pour batter into greased pan.
6. Bake for 22 to 25 minutes. Test center with toothpick making sure it comes out clean.
7. Allow cake to cool completely before soaking in Coffee Liqueur.

COFFEE LIQUEUR

1 cup	organic strong coffee grounds or espresso	3 cups	water
		1 ½ tbsp.	organic sugar

1. Brew the coffee using the grounds and water.
2. Once brewed, stir in the sugar until dissolved.
3. Place in fridge and allow coffee to cool completely before soaking the Ladyfingers.

MASCARPONE CREAM

1 ½ pounds	vegan cream cheese	1 tbsp.	vanilla extract
¾ cup	agave nectar		

Place all ingredients in a mixer or blender and mix well. Store in fridge until ready to use.

ASSEMBLY

1 recipe	Ladyfingers	1 recipe	Mascarpone Cream
1 recipe	Coffee Liqueur	¼ cup	chocolate shavings

1. Cut the cake into 12 pieces.
2. Dip the top half (horizontally) of each piece of cake into the Coffee Liqueur for 5 seconds.
3. Place dipped cake pieces in fridge, dipped side up, and allow to chill for 2 hours.
4. Top each piece with 2 ounces Mascarpone Cream and 1 teaspoon of chocolate shavings.

GARLIC BREAD

The rule is: *If you both eat garlic, you'll never taste it on each other.* So as long as both of you say, "I do," feel free to smother your taste buds with our garlic baguette.

RECIPE
Serves 4 to 6

ROASTED GARLIC AND GARLIC OIL
Makes about 2 cups

4 cups	garlic, peeled	2 cups	olive oil
1 tbsp.	sea salt	2 cups	vegetable oil
1 tsp.	ground black pepper		

1. Place garlic cloves in a small bowl and sprinkle salt and pepper over the cloves.
2. Pour both oils over the cloves.
3. Place all ingredients into a saucepan and simmer on medium-high heat for 35 to 40 minutes. Finished product should be a golden brown and not dark brown or black.
4. Strain oil into a separate container to cool. Final product should be 6 cups Garlic Oil and 2 cups of Roasted Garlic.
5. Remember to keep oil and cloves in the fridge, as they will spoil quickly at room temperature.

BREAD

½ cup	Roasted Garlic	3 tbsp.	Garlic Oil
1 whole	French baguette	2 tbsp.	parsley, minced

1. Place the Roasted Garlic in a food processor and blend into a purée.
2. Preheat oven to 350°F.
3. Cut the baguette in half lengthwise.
4. Drizzle the inside of both halves with the Garlic Oil.
5. Spread the purée evenly over both halves of baguette.
6. Bake the baguette for 12 to 14 minutes or until golden brown.
7. Cut each half into 4 pieces. Garnish with parsley.

TRUFFLE ASPARAGUS RISOTTO

Black truffle oil and vegan Parmesan join forces in this creamy dish that's sure to have your dinner mates swooning. Fun fact: Risotto is the method of cooking the rice in broth, not the name of the rice itself.

RECIPE

Makes 3 cups

PARMESAN

1 cup	raw cashews (almonds and walnuts work too)	½ tsp.	sea salt
¾ cup	nutritional yeast	½ tsp.	garlic powder

Place all ingredients in a dry food processor and blend until crumbly.

RISOTTO

2 tbsp.	safflower oil	3 tbsp.	vegan sour cream
½ cup	yellow onions, diced	1 tsp.	sea salt
¼ cup	shallots, diced	½ tsp.	ground black pepper
1 cup	Arborio rice	2 tbsp.	Parmesan
3 cups	warm water, or warm Vegetable Stock (page 17)	1 tbsp.	lemon zest
1 cup	asparagus, blanched, shocked in ice bath and chopped	1 tsp.	black truffle oil

1. Heat the safflower oil in a medium-sized saucepan. Add the onions and shallots and cook until translucent.
2. Add the rice and coat with the "fat" and natural onion juices for about 1 ½ minutes.
3. Add one cup of the water or stock and cook until almost dry.
4. Once the rice absorbs 80% of the liquid, add one more cup to the pot, along with the blanched asparagus.
5. When the rice is fully expanded, remove the pot from heat.
6. Add the vegan sour cream, sea salt, pepper, remaining Parmesan, lemon zest and truffle oil.

CAESAR SALAD

There are all sorts of foodies out there—savory foodies, sweet foodies and exotic foodies. Then there's a class all its own—Caesar Salad foodies. Some people order it off of every menu like they've been hit by the Caesar Cupid. We can't blame them, especially when it's done up vegan style. We've been hit, too!

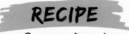

RECIPE
Serves 4 to 6

BALSAMIC GLAZE
Makes ¾ cups

3 cups	balsamic vinegar

1. Place the vinegar in a saucepan and cook at medium heat until reduced in volume by half.
2. Reduce the flame to low heat and allow the liquid to reduce by half again. The end product should have a thick syrup-like consistency and stick to the back of the spoon.

CAESAR DRESSING

1 clove	garlic, chopped	1 tsp.	yellow mustard
7 ounces	silken tofu	2 tbsp.	olive oil
1 tbsp.	lemon juice	¼ tsp.	sea salt
2 tbsp.	capers	¼ tsp.	ground black pepper
1 tbsp.	caper brine	½ cup	water
1 tsp.	organic sugar	½ cup	almonds, toasted and ground

1. Place all ingredients into the blender except for the ground almonds. Blend until smooth.
2. Pour the mixture into a small bowl and fold in the ground almonds.
3. Chill for 30 minutes before serving.

GARLIC CROUTONS

¼ cup	olive oil	1 pinch	sea salt
1 clove	garlic, peeled and pressed	2 buns	bread, day old
½ tsp.	paprika		

1. Preheat oven to 400°F.
2. In a blender, place the oil, garlic, paprika and salt and blend.
3. Cut day old buns into ½ x ½-inch pieces and place in a mixing bowl.
4. Drizzle the oil mixture over the bread and toss together. Mix well.
5. Place on a baking pan and bake until brown and crisp. At 4 minutes, remove from oven and flip croutons. To get even baking, put in for another 3 to 5 minutes. *Watch closely, croutons burn easily!*
6. Allow to cool on sheet pan.

ASSEMBLY

2 whole	romaine hearts	1 recipe	Balsamic Glaze
1 recipe	Caesar Dressing	½ cup	parsley, chopped
1 ½ cups	Garlic Croutons		

1. Remove the stem and cut ½ inch off the bottom of the romaine head.
2. Wash the leaves well.
3. Stack 4 to 5 leaves together on each plate.
4. Drizzle with Caesar Dressing and Balsamic Glaze.
5. Top with croutons and garnish with parsley.

HEART BEET SOUP

Heat things up before the main course with this steamy, heart-healthy beet soup that tastes as lavish as it sounds.

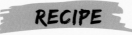

RECIPE

Serves 6 to 8 people

ROASTED RED BEETS	
3 pounds	red beets

1. Preheat the oven to 375°F.
2. Wrap each beet with foil, leaving the top open.
3. Place 2 tablespoons of water in each beet wrap and place on baking pan and roast.
4. The beets will take 55 to 65 minutes to roast.
5. When the beets are done, a toothpick will easily come out of the center.
6. Once roasted, allow to cool before cleaning.
7. Place roasted beets in a towel and "rub" the skin off until the beet is completely clean.
8. Rinse under warm water. Shred the beets with a cheese grater.

SOUP			
2 tbsp.	olive oil	6 cups	Roasted Red Beets
4 cloves	garlic, chopped	5 cups	Vegetable Stock (page 17)
2 tbsp.	fresh ginger, chopped	2 cups	orange juice
2 cups	leeks, diced and cleaned well	1 tbsp.	sea salt
		½ tsp.	pepper
2 cups	carrots, peeled and diced	to garnish	non-dairy sour cream

1. In a stockpot, heat the oil and add the garlic and ginger.
2. Add the leeks, carrots and beets. Cook on medium heat for about 2 minutes.
3. Pour in the Vegetable Stock and cook for another 3 to 4 minutes. Then add the orange juice, salt and pepper.
4. Remove from heat and let cool. Then blend in blender until smooth, in as many batches as necessary. Garnish with non-dairy sour cream (and make it into a heart shape like we did!).

NATIVE LASAGNA

What could be a more crush-worthy vegan meal than our Native Lasagna? It's a warm and romantic dish for your candlelit night in, or a perfect pass-around for a family celebration. It's love at first bite!

RECIPE

Makes 1 pan

NOODLES

1 box	vegan lasagna noodles

Prepare lasagna noodles according to package, making sure they are really al dente. If you're unsure, drain them early, as they will continue to cook in the oven.

SAUCE

1 medium	yellow onion, chopped	1 tbsp.	dried oregano
½ medium	red onion, chopped	1 tbsp.	dried basil
1 bulb	garlic, chopped	¾ cup	tomato paste
2 medium	carrots, chopped	15 oz	crushed tomatoes
3 stalks	celery, chopped	5 cups	tomato sauce
1 ½ tsp.	vegetable broth powder	¾ cup	dry red wine
3 links	seitan sausage, crumbled		

1. Place onions, garlic, carrots and celery in a large saucepot and fill with enough water to just barely cover the veggies. Add powdered broth and stir well.

2. Bring to boil, reduce heat to low and simmer for about 30 minutes, until the veggies get really soft. Liquid should be practically all gone.

3. Mash vegetables with a potato masher until veggies are mushy. Stir in seitan crumbles and herbs. Mix well over heat for a couple of minutes.

4. Stir in tomato paste and canned, crushed tomatoes. Continue to stir over heat for a couple of minutes.

5. Add in tomato sauce and wine and stir well.

6. Reduce heat to medium-low and let simmer for about 30 more minutes or until sauce is nice and thick.

TOFU RICOTTA

2- 14 ounce boxes	silken tofu, firm or extra-firm and pressed to remove liquid	4 tbsp.	lemon juice
		¼ cup	nutritional yeast
		½ cup	Kalamata olives, chopped
15 ounces	white beans, drained and rinsed	½ cup	vegan mozzarella, shredded
		to taste	sea salt and pepper

1. In a large mixing bowl, combine tofu and beans and mash well.
2. Add lemon juice, yeast, olives, mozzarella cheese, salt and pepper. Mix well.

ASSEMBLY

¼ cup	mozzarella cheese

1. Preheat oven to 350°F.
2. Grease a 13 x 9-inch baking pan and place ⅓ of the sauce to cover the bottom. Cover with a layer of noodles and ¼ of the ricotta. Repeat two or three more times, with the noodles, sauce and ricotta.
3. Sprinkle the top layer with mozzarella cheese.
4. Bake lasagna for about 30 minutes. You can broil the top for a few minutes at the end if you'd like.

CARDAMOM ROSE CUPCAKES

*R*oses are red, violets are blue,this Native favorite we give unto you.
Cookies and chocolate may well be passé,
So try these new cupcakes on Valentine's Day.
The cardamom gives them a spicy-sweet kick,
And rose water frosting you may want to lick.
So relish this special East Indian treat,
And make sure to leave at least some for your sweet!

RECIPE
Makes 18 cupcakes

ROSE FROSTING			
1 cup	vegan shortening	2 tbsp.	rose water
1 cup	vegan margarine	4 cups	powdered sugar

1. Place shortening and margarine in a mixing bowl and beat until well-combined and fluffy, about 3 minutes using a hand mixer.
2. Add rose water and gradually add powdered sugar (approximately ½-cup add-ins). Stop occasionally to scrape sides of the bowl and beat about three minutes.
3. Scoop into a pastry bag with tip (or quart sized Ziploc with tip cut, so you can squeeze the frosting out to draw with it) or into a bowl to spread with spatula. Set aside.

CUPCAKES

2 ¼ cups	unbleached organic flour	½ tsp.	cardamom, ground
1 ¼ cups	organic sugar	½ cup	safflower oil
2 tsp.	baking powder	1 ½ cups	rice milk
½ tsp.	baking soda	1 tbsp.	apple cider vinegar
½ tsp.	sea salt	2 tsp.	vanilla extract

1. Sift dry ingredients including flour, sugar, baking powder, baking soda, sea salt and cardamom.
2. In large mixing bowl, place dry mix and create a "well" for the wet ingredients. Set aside.
3. Place all wet ingredients in a small bowl and mix well using a whisk.
4. Add the liquid to the dry ingredients using a whisk to incorporate.
5. Place liners in the cupcake pan and fill each compartment leaving ¼ inch from the top empty.
6. Bake cupcakes for 15 to 17 minutes at 325°F, or until a toothpick comes out clean. Let cool for 2 hours.
7. Take a cupcake and, using the filled pastry bag, place a large ¼ cup rosette on top.

GO GREEN

- St. Paddy's Day Melt
- Shepherd's Pie
- Luck of the Irish Whoopie Pies
- Fresh Peas with Mint and Chives
- Creamy Potato Salad with Bacon
- Vegan Irish Cream

Everyone seems to feel the "luck of the Irish" on St. Paddy's Day, so why not go all the way green while you're at it? Per the Irish tradition, the celebration is an official day of feasting, so naturally we're prepping you with a host of Celtic flavors. And thanking our lucky clovers for them!

From the top o' the mornin' the streets will be spilling over with festive parade-goers and rowdy partiers, all melded together in one sea of green. Find solace from the madness in your kitchen, where you can whip up Shepherd's Pie and Potato Pancakes for your happy, but hungry, friends.

ST. PADDY'S DAY MELT

Leaping Leprechaun, this melt is magic! Stack this pile o' gold high on toasted rye with blackened seitan, melted vegan cheddar and horseradish sauce. It's a fun way for guests to munch in between festivities and stay out of mischief with their hungry stomachs.

RECIPE
Makes 8 melts

MARINATED SEITAN

1 tbsp.	ginger, chopped and peeled	1 tsp.	sea salt
1 tbsp.	garlic, chopped	2 pounds	Peppered Seitan (Original Seitan recipe on page 41 with 2 tsp. garlic powder, 4 tsp. crackled black peppercorns, 2 tsp. onion powder, all added in first step of recipe), sliced
1 cup	orange juice		
¼ cup	lemon juice		
1 tsp.	smoked paprika		
1 tbsp.	chili powder		
¼ cup	rice vinegar		

1. In a mixing bowl, add all ingredients except the Peppered Seitan. Whisk well.
2. Pour the marinade over the sliced seitan and mix together.
3. Let it marinate for 12 hours in the refrigerator.

CARAMELIZED ONIONS
Makes 2 cups

4 pounds	yellow onions, cut in half and peeled	1 tsp.	sea salt
⅓ cup	olive oil	½ tsp.	ground white pepper
		1 tbsp.	maple syrup

1. Place halved onions in food processor and slice using the thinnest blade or slice by hand in ¼-inch pieces.
2. Heat oil in skillet and add onions and salt.
3. At medium-high heat, cook and stir until transparent and lightly brown.
4. Turn to low heat and mix with tongs.
5. Remove from heat and mix in white pepper and maple syrup.

STEAMED KALE

1 bunch	kale

1. Fill bottom of a double boiler with 2 inches of water and bring to boil.
2. In the meantime, remove stems and cut into 2 ½ x 2 ½-inch pieces.
3. Place the kale in the steamer insert and cover. Steam for 5 minutes.
4. Remove from steamer, shock in ice bath and dry.

BEET HORSERADISH SAUCE

¼ cup	Roasted Red Beets (page 75), shredded	1 tsp.	Dijon mustard
		2 tbsp.	green onions, chopped
1 cup	vegan mayo	2 tsp.	fresh dill, finely sliced
⅓ cup	fresh horseradish or non-dairy jarred horseradish	1 half	lemon, zested

Combine all ingredients together in a bowl and whisk together.

ASSEMBLY
Makes 1 melt

2 slices	rye bread	1 ounce	vegan cheddar cheese
1 tsp.	olive oil	1 tbsp.	vegan mayo
½ cup	Marinated Seitan	1 cup	Steamed Kale (page 86)
2 tbsp.	Caramelized Onions (page 85)	¼ cup	Beet Horseradish Sauce

1. Heat sauté pan and brush each side of rye bread with olive oil.
2. Toast each side of the bread until golden brown.
3. In a small sauté pan, heat the Marinated Seitan for about 2 ½ minutes or until hot.
4. Place hot onions on the Marinated Seitan and cover with a slice of cheese. Melt the cheese using a cover.
5. Place one tablespoon of mayo on the bottom of one piece of rye bread. Then add patty.
6. Add steamed kale to the top of the cheese. Spread Beet Horseradish Sauce on the other half of bread. Top the sandwich.
7. Devour!

SHEPHERD'S PIE

"**C**ottage Pie" would be a tad more fitting for St. Patrick's Day, since it uses beef (as the Irish did) instead of lamb (like a Shepherd's Pie). But we took the meat out altogether, so Shepherd's Pie it is!

RECIPE

Serves 6 to 8

MASHED POTATOES

1 pound	russet potatoes, peeled and chopped	2 tsp.	ground black pepper
¼ cup	vegan butter	2 tsp.	sea salt

1. Place the potato pieces in a pot of water and bring to a boil. Once it begins to boil, reduce to a simmer for 30 minutes or until tender.
2. When the potatoes are done, strain them and place them back in the pot. Add the butter, pepper and salt. Mash and set aside.

FILLING

1 tbsp.	olive oil	¾ cup	non-dairy milk
4 cloves	garlic, minced	2 tsp.	poultry seasoning
1 cup	yellow onion, diced	2 tsp.	garlic powder
1 ½ cups	carrots, peeled and diced	2 tsp.	ground black pepper
1 cup	parsnips, peeled and diced	2 tsp.	sea salt
4 stalks	celery, diced	2 tbsp.	fresh thyme, chopped
1 cup	Vegetable Stock (page 17), or water	2 tbsp.	unbleached organic flour

1. Preheat the oven to 425°F. Grease a casserole dish.
2. Heat the oil in a skillet on medium-high heat. Add the minced garlic and chopped onion. Cook for about 3 minutes. Add the carrots, parsnips and celery. Cook for 3 more minutes. Reduce the heat to low.
3. Add the flour to the pan and coat the veggies well.
4. Whisk the stock and milk together with the seasonings and spices.
5. Add the liquid mix to the pan and whisk in well. Cook for another 7 to 10 minutes or until the mix becomes thick. Season to taste.
6. Pour the veggie mix into the pan. Allow the mix to cool before adding in the mashed potatoes. Spread the mashed potatoes over the mix with a spatula.
7. Bake for about 25 to 27 minutes or until golden on the top and bubbling on the sides. Allow pie to cool for 10 minutes before serving.

LUCK OF THE IRISH WHOOPIE PIES

Whoopie! Two soft chocolate cookies + one layer of thick mint frosting = a dozen guests asking for seconds. These melt-in-your-mouth, handheld desserts are sure to put you and your party over the rainbow.

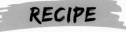

RECIPE

Makes 16 pies

PIE

1 ¾ cups	unbleached organic flour	2 tbsp.	egg replacer (no water)
¾ cup	cocoa powder	4 tbsp.	vegan butter, soft
½ tsp.	baking soda	¼ cup	vegan shortening, soft
½ tsp.	sea salt	1 cup	soy milk
1 cup	brown sugar	½ tsp.	vanilla extract

1. Sift all dry ingredients together and add to mixing bowl.
2. On medium speed, add the butter and mix for 30 seconds.
3. Add the shortening and mix for 30 seconds.
4. Add all liquid ingredients and mix until well incorporated.
5. Using a spoon or ice cream scoop, scoop and drop cookie portions onto an oiled cookie sheet.
6. Bake at 350°F for 10 to 15 minutes. Allow them to cool completely before frosting.

Egg replacer is a vegan alternative to eggs that is great
for baking. This gluten-free product, made from potato starch and
tapioca flour, adds moisture to cakes and helps flour rise.
With friends like that, who needs eggs?

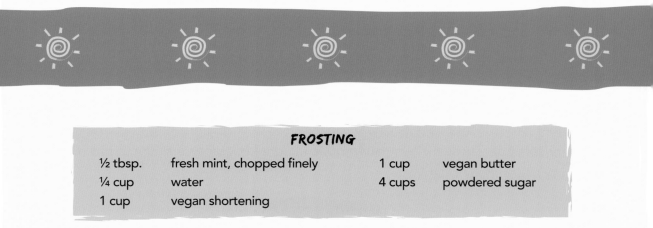

FROSTING

½ tbsp.	fresh mint, chopped finely	1 cup	vegan butter
¼ cup	water	4 cups	powdered sugar
1 cup	vegan shortening		

1. Blend the mint with the water in a blender until smooth.
2. In a mixer, on medium speed, mix the shortening and butter together until smooth, about 2 minutes.
3. Turn the speed down to low, and slowly add the sugar (½ cup at a time). Once all sugar is added, add the mint purée.
4. Frost in between cookies.

FRESH PEAS WITH MINT AND CHIVES

*O*ur fresh take on this vegetable will taste great to the sound of bagpipes and whistles. Plus, in the midst of parade ruckus and proud Irish banter, who could turn down world peas?

RECIPE
Serves 6 to 8

2 pounds	English peas	6 leaves	mint, chopped
1 or 2 whole	shallots, peeled and thinly sliced	¼ cup	chives, chopped
1 tbsp.	olive oil	¼ tsp.	sea salt

1. Bring a large pot of water to boil.
2. Cook peas in boiling water for about 2 minutes, drain and place in an ice bath to "shock" and keep them bright green.
3. In a skillet, sauté shallots in olive oil until soft, brown and lightly caramelized.
4. Move shallots and olive oil into bowl with peas and toss with mint leaves, chives and salt.

CREAMY POTATO SALAD WITH BACON

*O*ne potato, two potatoes, more more more! We're bringing this bacon-infused potato salad with us everywhere, including the parade route this holiday. Our vegan version keeps well, so it's ready for the road wherever the festivities take you.

RECIPE

Serves 4 to 6

1 pound	Yukon Gold potatoes, diced into 1-inch pieces	¼ cup	vegan mayo
		1 tsp.	sea salt
¼ cup	green onions, chopped	2 tbsp.	apple cider vinegar
¼ cup	red onions, diced	¼ tsp.	ground black pepper
1 cup	Native Bacon (page 23), diced	1 tsp.	agave syrup

1. Dice potatoes into 1-inch squares.
2. Place potatoes in a large pot with water and bring to a boil. Cook for 15 to 17 minutes. Check to make sure potatoes are not crunchy or mushy.
3. Rinse potatoes to stop cooking process.
4. Place the potatoes in a mixing bowl. Add all the other ingredients and mix gently with a large spoon.

We're a wee bit obsessed with this Irish tradition and we love it even better the vegan way, with coconut milk, brown sugar and whiskey. It's the perfect way to add a little jig to your step at your St. Paddy's celebration.

RECIPE

Serves 4 to 6

13 ½ ounces	coconut milk	1 ½ tsp.	pure vanilla extract
2 tbsp.	brown sugar	⅓ cup	strong coffee or coffee liqueur
¼ cup	non-dairy creamer (try the hazelnut)	½ to ¾ cup	whiskey (or to taste)

1. Combine all ingredients in blender and blend until smooth, or whisk together in a bowl.
2. Add more sugar or more whiskey to preference.
3. Keep refrigerated. It will last about two weeks.

Add chocolate syrup for extra sweetness.

BIG EASY BASH

- Old Bayou Tempeh Cakes
- Drunken Beans
- Mardi Gras Apple Punch
- Bananas Foster Shooters
- Portobello Po' Boy
- Gumbolaya

No one does Mardi Gras quite like, or even close to, New Orleans. But just because you don't live in NOLA doesn't mean you can't enjoy this peculiar holiday of masked costumes, figurine babies in cakes and all-out madness in the streets of the Big Easy.

We love Mardi Gras not only for the colorful beads and spirited parades, but also for the taste of Louisiana's traditional grub. Plus we pounce on any chance to veganize ethnic cuisine. We're guessing you do, too.

OLD BAYOU TEMPEH CAKES

Sitting where the Mississippi River hits the Gulf, New Orleans is rich with history, culture and unique food—especially seafood. The peppers, cilantro and cayenne pepper work in harmony to jazz up this fishless dish and our addicting Chipotle Remoulade sauce will have you singing for more.

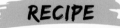

RECIPE
Makes 12 cakes

CHIPOTLE REMOULADE

1 cup	vegan mayo	2 tbsp.	red peppers, diced
2 tbsp.	red onion, diced	½ tbsp.	chipotle chili purée (blend can of chipotle peppers with its juice)
2 tbsp.	capers, drained		

Place all ingredients in a bowl and mix together.

CAKES

1 pound	tempeh (any store-bought tempeh), room temperature	¼ cup	cilantro, chopped
		1 whole	lemon, zested
		1 tsp.	sea salt
¼ cup	red peppers, diced	1 tsp.	cayenne pepper
¼ cup	red onion, diced	½ tsp.	garlic powder
¼ cup	scallions, sliced	¾ tsp.	cumin
¼ cup	parsley, chopped	2 tbsp.	olive oil

1. Place tempeh in food processor or a similar device and process until fine and sticky. Should only take 20 to 25 minutes.
2. Transfer into a bowl and add peppers, onions, scallion, herbs and seasonings. Mix very well.
3. Form mixture by using a scoop or just make little patties in your hands. Round out the sides and flatten the top and bottom for searing.
4. Heat olive oil in a sauté pan over medium-high heat. Add patties, flat side down and allow them to get a nice sear and golden brown color. Flip over the cake and repeat on other side.
5. Serve warm with Chipotle Remoulade.

DRUNKEN BEANS

*T*hese kidney and pinto beans must be drunk the way they're dancing around this dark beer and oregano sauce. Join the fun and slurp up some of this hearty entrée—no need for restraint on a day like today.

RECIPE

Serves 4 to 5

1 cup	white onions, diced	1 ½ cups	dark beer or Vegetable Stock (page 17)
¼ cup	jalapeño, diced with seeds		
2 tbsp.	water (to sauté)	2 cups	tomatoes, diced
1 can	pinto beans, rinsed and drained	1 ½ tbsp.	dried oregano
		1 tsp.	sea salt
1 can	kidney beans, rinsed and drained	1 cup	cilantro, chopped
		1 tbsp.	lime zest

1. Sauté the onions and diced jalapeño in 2 tablespoons of water for about 1 minute.
2. Add both beans and cook for 1 minute.
3. Add the beer (or stock) and allow the alcohol to cook out. This will take about 8 to 10 minutes on medium heat.
4. When the beer has reduced by half, add the diced tomatoes, dried oregano and sea salt. Cook for 10 to 12 minutes. The ingredients should be getting thick.
5. Remove the pan from the heat and finish with the cilantro and lime zest.

MARDI GRAS APPLE PUNCH

Sweeten up this spicy holiday with our original red apple punch. Serve it to post-parade guests and let the dancing begin.

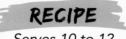

RECIPE
Serves 10 to 12

16 whole	apples, cored but not peeled, juiced	24 ounces	sparkling white grape juice or champagne
1 cup	lemon juice, freshly squeezed	2 whole	apples, thinly sliced
		2 whole	lemons, thinly sliced
4 cups	orange juice, freshly squeezed	2 whole	oranges, thinly sliced

1. In a large pitcher or punch bowl, combine the apple and lemon juice immediately after juicing to keep the apples pink. Stir in the orange juice, cover and chill.
2. Just before serving, add the sparkling white grape juice or champagne and sliced fruit garnish.

BANANAS FOSTER SHOOTERS

The Big Easy lays sole claim to this rum-infused dessert, which was first conceived in 1951 at an upscale New Orleans restaurant. It's named after Richard Foster of the New Orleans Crime Commission, but these bananas are so wildly good, they must be breaking a law.

RECIPE

Makes 12 mini shooters (2 ounce glasses)

CAKE

2 tsp.	egg replacer	2 ounces	silken tofu, firm and buzzed
¼ cup	warm water		
2 tsp.	safflower oil	¼ cup	safflower oil
1 cup	unbleached organic flour	¼ cup	soy milk
¾ cup	organic cane sugar	½ tsp.	vanilla extract
2 tbsp.	baking powder	¼ cup	dark rum
2 tsp.	sea salt	¼ cup	vegan butter (room temperature)

1. Preheat the oven to 325°F. Grease a 9 x 13-inch cake pan with safflower oil.
2. In a small bowl, whisk the 'eggs' with the warm water until fluffy. Takes about 1 minute. Set aside.
3. Combine the flour, sugar, baking powder and salt and sift together. Fold in butter, mix will be crumbly using your hands or a fork.
4. Place the tofu, oil, soy milk, vanilla extract and rum in the blender and blend until smooth.
5. Slowly add the wet ingredients to the dry mix, a little at a time. Mix until the batter is lump free.

Generally, all liquors are vegan friendly. It's just the beers and wines that may not be. Check out http://www.barnivore.com/ just to be safe!

6. Slowly fold in the fluffy 'egg' mix. This will only take 15 seconds. Be careful not to over mix.

7. Pour the batter into the greased pan and bake for 25 to 30 minutes, or until the toothpick is clean.

8. Allow the cake to cool before assembling the shooters.

PUDDING

1 cup	unsweetened soy milk	½ cup	organic cane sugar
2 tsp.	vanilla extract	14 ounces	silken tofu
¼ tsp.	rum extract (or ½ tsp. rum)	2 whole	bananas, ripe, diced for purée
¼ tsp.	sea salt		

1. Place the soy milk, vanilla, rum and sea salt in a small pan on medium heat.

2. Whisk until the sugar dissolves.

3. Once dissolved, remove the pot from the heat and pour the mixture into a blender. Add the tofu and 2 diced bananas. Blend until smooth.

4. Allow the pudding to cool before portioning.

ASSEMBLY

1 recipe	Pudding	2 whole	bananas, sliced thinly
1 recipe	Cake	12 sprigs	fresh mint

1. Place 1 tablespoon of pudding in the bottom of each 2-ounce shooter glass.
2. Cut the cooled cake into 24 equal cube or round pieces. Place 1 piece of cake on top of the pudding, followed by 2 slices of banana.
3. Next, place 1 tablespoon of pudding on top of each banana piece, and follow with 1 piece of cake.
4. Finish the shooter with 1 tablespoon of pudding.
5. Garnish with a final slice of banana and a fresh sprig of mint.
6. Serve immediately—bananas will oxidize and change colors, as bananas do!

PORTOBELLO PO' BOY

The Po'boy is a traditional Louisianan sub-sandwich made with roast beef or seafood, but we prefer ours with battered shrooms. Plus the sub is mostly known for the heavenly French-style baguette. We're definitely not "sub"-stituting that!

RECIPE

Makes 1 Po' Boy

BATTERED MUSHROOMS
Makes 4 pieces

2 cups	unsweetened, organic coconut milk	1 pound	Grilled Portobello Mushrooms (page 120)
2 cups	unbleached organic flour	3 cups	vegetable oil

1. Place a piece of parchment paper on the bottom of a sheet pan to cover.
2. In one bowl place the milk and in another bowl place the flour.
3. Saturate the 1 mushroom piece in milk, and then place it in the flour fully covering.
4. Dip the mushroom again into the milk and once again into the flour.
5. Place the piece onto a sheet pan.
6. Heat oil to 350°F. Place one mushroom in oil at a time. Cook 3 to 3 ½ minutes or until golden brown. Then repeat with remaining mushrooms.

ASSEMBLY

1 each	French bread (12 inches)	½ cup	romaine, shredded
1 tsp.	Garlic Oil (page 69)	3 whole	Roma tomatoes, sliced
¼ cup	Chipotle Remoulade (page 99)	4 whole	dill pickle slices
		1 tsp.	fresh parsley, chopped
4 whole	Battered Mushrooms		

1. Brush the bread with Garlic Oil and place in a sauté pan on medium-high heat for 2 to 3 minutes or until toasted.
2. Spread ¼ cup Chipotle Remoulade on the bottom of the bread.
3. Once the mushrooms are done, layer them across the remoulade, slightly overlapping.
4. Place ½ cup of romaine lettuce on the mushrooms. Then layer the tomato slices and dill pickle slices on top of the lettuce. Sprinkle with parsley. Dig in!

GUMBOLAYA

ew Orleans sure isn't N'awlins without its gumbo. And with this vegan recipe, you can bring the same seafood flavors of "Fisherman's Paradise" right into the mouths and bellies of your guests.

RECIPE

Serves 6 to 8

¼ cup	water (for sautéing)		1 tbsp.	garlic powder
2 cloves	garlic, minced		2 whole	bay leaves
1 cup	carrots, washed and diced		½ tsp.	ground black pepper
1 cup	celery, diced		1 tbsp.	sea salt
1 cup	yellow onions, diced		1 quart	water
1 cup	red peppers, diced		1 medium	zucchini, diced in ½-inch pieces
1 cup	tomato paste		1 cup	Roma tomatoes, diced
2 cups	organic brown rice		½ pound	tempeh, diced
1 tsp.	dry oregano		½ pound	Original Seitan (page 41), diced
1 tsp.	smoked hot paprika			
½ tsp.	cayenne pepper			

So what's the difference between a gumbo and a jambalaya? A gumbo is served over rice with a roux and usually contains okra and a filé spice. Jambalayas have rice mixed in, no roux or okra.

1. Place the ¼ cup of water in a large soup pot. Add the garlic, carrots, celery and onion. Sauté them for 3 minutes on medium-high heat.
2. Add the red peppers and the tomato paste. Cook for 3 more minutes.
3. Add the brown rice, spices, bay leaves, black pepper and salt.
4. Add the water and bring to a boil. Then turn the heat down to a simmer.
5. Simmer for 20 minutes on low.
6. Add the zucchini, tomatoes, tempeh and seitan. Simmer for 20 to 25 more minutes on low heat, or until the rice is cooked all the way. You may need to add more water if the rice isn't done. The end consistency should be nice and thick.
7. Remove the bay leaves, check the seasoning and adjust if needed.

SPRING FLING

- Fresh Asparagus Avocado Salad
- Moroccan Pickled Carrots
- Spring Wellington
- Coconut Lime Cake
- Spring Waldorf Salad
- Soba Noodle Salad
- Orange Dreamsicle Cupcakes
- Spring Snap Pea Salad

*I*t's finally time to change our clocks and spring forward into long, sunny days and warm breezes. Spring fever sets into our jubilant hearts and, more importantly, our rejuvenated backyards (or raised beds, or rooftop havens, or community gardens). Trees bloom, buds blossom and our stew-laden tongues taste the scent of fresh pickin's.

This bouquet of recipes includes light, refreshing bites after a sleepy, sedentary winter. We made sure that for whatever occasion you're celebrating, you serve the most revitalizing finds you can get your gardening gloves on. Now move over winter, spring has sprung!

FRESH ASPARAGUS AVOCADO SALAD

Asparagus is the first veggie to poke its purplish head out of the dirt come spring. The event is essentially the vegan version of Groundhog's Day, but with a 100% forecast of a happy ending.

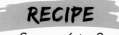

RECITPE

Serves 6 to 8

½ gallon	water	1 tbsp.	mint, chopped
½ tsp.	sea salt	1 tbsp.	balsamic vinegar
2 pounds	asparagus, ends removed, cut into 2-inch pieces	1 tsp.	maple syrup
		½ tsp.	sea salt
¼ cup	olive oil	1 pinch	ground black pepper
1 whole	lemon, juiced and zested	2 whole	avocados cut in ½-inch cubes
2 tbsp.	Italian parsley, chopped		
1 tbsp.	cilantro, chopped		

1. Bring 2 quarts of water to boil with salt.
2. Drop in asparagus and let cook about 3 minutes.
3. Immediately drain and shock in ice bath. Set aside.
4. In a small bowl, whisk together the rest of the ingredients, except the avocado.
5. Toss with asparagus and avocado.

We love this dish over grains like rice or quinoa, or inside a crusty roll for a unique sandwich filling.

MOROCCAN PICKLED CARROTS

Here's the chic (and way more delish) version of your grandmother's lukewarm cooked carrots. We serve ours chilled, pickled with chiles, topped with maple syrup and cinnamon and, of course, in classic mason jars.

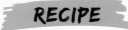
RECIPE

Makes two 16-ounce mason jars

1½ pounds	carrots, peeled		¼ cup	organic sugar or maple syrup
4 cloves	garlic, sliced			
3 small	dried arbol chiles, cut in half		1 ½ tbsp.	sea salt
			2 tsp.	coriander seeds
1 whole	lemon, peel only		2 tsp.	cumin seeds
1½ cups	water		1 stick	cinnamon
1 cup	apple cider vinegar			

1. Cut carrots on a diagonal into ¼-inch slices.
2. Tightly pack into a mason jar.
3. Add garlic, chilies and lemon peel.
4. Quickly pulse coriander, cumin and cinnamon in a blender or spice mill until the seeds are just barely cracked.
5. Mix water, vinegar, sugar and salt in a sauce pan and bring to boil. Let boil for two minutes.
6. Pour over carrots. Add spices.
7. Cool and cover jar tightly for a minimum of 12 hours. Serve chilled. These will keep for a week in the fridge!

SPRING WELLINGTON

And now ladies and gentlemen, our feature presentation...It's the crown jewel of vegan cuisine, the Eighth Wonder of the World...It's the Spring Wellington! Packed with veggies and exploding with flavor, it's the motherboard of your spring celebration and it always has guests oohing and ahhing.

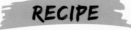

RECIPE

Serves 6 to 8

GREEN PEAS, CORN AND SHALLOTS

1 tbsp.	olive oil		½ tsp.	sea salt
½ cup	shallots, sliced		1 cup	green peas, thawed
1 tsp.	dry tarragon		1 cup	corn kernels, thawed

1. In a sauté pan, heat olive oil and sauté shallots until transparent and lightly browned.
2. Add tarragon and salt.
3. Remove from heat and place into a mixing bowl.
4. Add peas and corn, stir together.

LEMON HOLLANDAISE SAUCE

1 tbsp.	olive oil		⅛ tsp.	turmeric spice
1 whole	shallot, peeled and diced		⅛ tsp.	ground white pepper
1 cup	soy milk		⅛ tsp.	cayenne spice
½ cup	lemon juice		2 tbsp.	tapioca starch
1 tsp.	dry tarragon		½ cup	water
½ tsp.	sea salt			

1. Heat oil in pot and sauté shallots until transparent and lightly browned.
2. Add soy milk, lemon juice, tarragon, salt, turmeric, white pepper and cayenne. Whisk together and let simmer for 10 minutes, stirring frequently.
3. Dissolve tapioca starch in the water with a whisk.
4. Bring sauce to low boil and add tapioca mix.
5. Cook until thickened 2 to 3 minutes.

MASHED POTATOES

½ pound	Yukon Gold potatoes	4 cloves	Roasted Garlic (page 69)
⅛ cup	Garlic Oil (page 69)	1 tsp.	sea salt
¼ cup	soy milk	½ tsp.	garlic powder

1. Rinse and peel potatoes.
2. Cut in half and steam for 25 minutes.
3. Add remaining ingredients and mash the potatoes.
4. Whisk mixture until peaks form in mashed potatoes.

GRILLED PORTOBELLO

4 large	portobello mushrooms	½ tsp.	sea salt
1 tbsp.	Garlic Oil (page 69)		

1. Wash mushroom caps. With the stems facing up, slice the mushrooms into ½-inch slices (about 6 to 10 slices per mushroom).
2. Place portobello slices in a large bowl and toss with the oil and salt.
3. Place the sliced mushrooms in a fry pan and grill for 2 ½ minutes, then flip and rotate with tongs. Repeat on the other side for 2 ½ more minutes.
4. Repeat with other half of the mushrooms.
5. Lay mushrooms in a single layer on a sheet pan and complete the cooling process.

ASSEMBLY

1 sheet	puff pastry	4 each	carrots, peeled and sliced
1 handful	unbleached organic flour (for rolling)	½ cup	Grilled Portobello
1 cup	Steamed Kale (page 86)	¼ pound	Original Seitan (page 41), sliced
¾ cup	Mashed Potatoes	1 cup	Lemon Hollandaise Sauce
½ cup	Green Peas, Corn and Shallots		

1. Place the puff pastry on a floured piece of parchment or plastic wrap. (That will help with the rolling.)
2. Place the Steamed Kale along the bottom of the puff pastry leaving about 3 inches from the bottom and 2 inches on both sides, so you will be able to roll the pastry.
3. Place the mashed potato on top of the kale and spread evenly.
4. Put the Green Peas, Corn and Shallots on top of the mashed potatoes. Follow with the seitan.
5. Place the thinly sliced carrots on top of the pea mix.
6. Top the carrots with the Grilled Portobello.
7. Holding the edge of the parchment paper, carefully hold the ingredients together with the paper while rolling (like sushi).
8. Secure by pressing the ends of the puff pastry together and also rolling under each side as well.
9. Brush with olive oil and place on lined baking sheet.
10. With a knife, make 4 slits on a diagonal along the top. Bake at 425°F for 45 to 55 minutes. Drizzle with Hollandaise or use it as a dip.

COCONUT LIME CAKE

Election year or not, we've got an age-old debate. Cake or pie? The lime zest, toasted coconut topping, and uh-maze-ing frosting on this cake have pie people taking a hard right (or would it be left?) to the other side.

RECIPE

Makes 1 cake

TOASTED COCONUT

½ cup	shredded coconut

1. Heat skillet over medium-high heat.
2. Add shredded coconut to a dry hot skillet, sauté.
3. Toast for 2 to 3 minutes until golden brown, then cool

COCONUT LIME FROSTING

½ cup	vegan shortening	1 tsp.	coconut extract (alcohol free)
½ cup	vegan butter	2 tbsp.	lime juice
2 cups	powdered sugar		

1. Place shortening in a mixer and mix with the whisk attachment for 2 minutes, or until smooth and lump free.
2. Add the butter and whisk until incorporated
3. Add powdered sugar, 1 cup at a time, until frosting is light and fluffy—about 2 minutes.
4. Add coconut extract and lime juice and mix for 30 more seconds.

COCONUT LIME CAKE

1 tsp.	vegan butter	1 cup	soy milk
1 ½ cups	unbleached organic flour	¼ cup	lime juice
½ tbsp.	baking powder	1 tsp.	coconut extract
¼ tsp.	sea salt	1 tsp.	vanilla extract
¾ cup	organic sugar	1 tsp.	lime zest

1. Grease 9 x 13-inch pan with vegan butter.
2. Preheat oven to 350°F.
3. In a bowl, whisk together all dry ingredients.
4. Combine all liquid ingredients together in container.
5. Slowly add the liquid to dry ingredients and mix well. Fold in lime zest.
6. Bake for 18 to 20 minutes.
7. Allow the cake to cool completely before frosting.

ASSEMBLY

1 recipe	Coconut Lime Cake	½ cup	Toasted Coconut
1 recipe	Coconut Lime Frosting	2 tsp.	lime zest

1. Frost cooled lime cake with 2 cups of frosting.
2. Top cake with ½ cup toasted coconuts and 2 teaspoons of lime zest.
3. Allow to cool completely before portioning.

SPRING WALDORF SALAD

This salad first appeared in the 1890s at the Waldorf Hotel in New York City and was the quintessence of elegance. Now, every household recipe box has its own variation of the salad (because it's so darn good!). So what's a cookbook without one? We *had* to share ours.

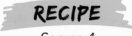
RECIPE
Serves 4

SPELT BERRIES

2 cups	spelt berries		6 cups	water

1. Soak spelt berries in water overnight.
2. Cook on medium heat for about an hour. Drain.

PEAR GINGER MINT VINAIGRETTE

¼ cup	mint leaves, loosely packed		⅔ cup	sunflower or safflower oil
			½ tsp.	ginger, finely minced
⅓ cup	pear vinegar		¼ tsp.	sea salt

Chop mint leaves, then in a bowl, whisk together with vinegar, oil, ginger and salt.

MAPLE GLAZED NUT CRUNCH

¾ cup	pecan halves		3 tbsp.	maple syrup
¾ cup	walnut halves		1 tbsp.	brown sugar
1 tbsp.	vegan margarine		1 pinch	sea salt

1. Put nuts in heated skillet on medium temperature and stir until they are toasted and lightly browned.
2. Add margarine and toss nuts to coat.
3. Stir in maple syrup, sugar and salt.
4. Reduce flame and stir until nuts are toasted and liquid is gone.
5. Let cool on parchment paper so walnuts don't clump.

ASSEMBLY

8 cups	romaine lettuce leaves, torn	1 cup	dried cherries
2 cups	Spelt Berries	½ cup	Pear Ginger Mint Vinaigrette
2 cups	apples, diced	1 ½ cups	Maple Glazed Nut Crunch
1 cup	organic celery, thinly sliced	4 tbsp.	chives, finely chopped

1. In a large bowl toss together the first 5 ingredients with vinaigrette.
2. Garnish with Maple Glazed Nut Crunch and chopped chives.

SOBA NOODLE SALAD

We understand that eating (and twirling!) noodles at parties can get a little awkward, but with this fun and colorful Asian-inspired dish, you'll have all of your guests slurping together.

RECIPE

Serves 6 people

2 pounds	soba noodles	2 cups	red bell peppers, diced
2 tbsp.	sesame oil	2 cups	snap peas, julienned
1 tbsp.	garlic, chopped	6 tbsp.	soy sauce
1 tbsp.	ginger, chopped	2 tbsp.	rice vinegar
2 cups	yellow onions, diced	1 cup	cilantro, chopped
2 cups	Japanese eggplant, julienned	1 tbsp.	sesame seeds
2 cups	shitake mushrooms, julienned	1 tbsp.	hot chili sauce

1. Bring 1 gallon of water to a boil.
2. Add the soba noodles and cook for 10 minutes until soft.
3. Remove from heat and strain, then pass through cold water.
4. Add the sesame oil to prevent from sticking.
5. In a 10-inch sauté pan, sauté the garlic and ginger with sesame oil and brown them for about 10 seconds, stirring constantly so nothing burns.
6. Begin to add the vegetables. Add the onion first so that the sweetness comes out as they caramelize. Then add the eggplant, mushrooms, red bell peppers and peas.
7. Once all the vegetables are added and mixed with the noodles, begin to add your sauces. Pour in the soy sauce, rice vinegar, chopped cilantro, sesame seeds and chili sauce. Then enjoy this amazingly flavorful dish!

ORANGE DREAMSICLE CUPCAKES

*T*his dessert's flavors remind us of ice cream trucks, drippy popsicles and sticky fingers. But don't wait until summer for the tune of "Pop Goes the Weasel" floating down your street to feel nostalgic. Bite into these dreamy 'cakes instead.

RECIPE
Makes 18 cupcakes

ORANGE CREAM

1 cup	vegan cream cheese	1 each	orange zest
½ cup	vegan sour cream	½ cup	powdered sugar

1. Place all ingredients in mixer and mix well with whisk.
2. Portion 2 tablespoons into each cupcake using a piping bag or a resealable bag with a cut tip.

VANILLA FROSTING

1 cup	vegan shortening	4 tbsp.	vanilla extract
1 cup	vegan butter	4 cups	powdered sugar

1. Place shortening and butter in mixer using the whisk attachment and whisk until well-combined and fluffy, about 3 minutes.
2. Add vanilla, then gradually add powdered sugar. Stop occasionally to scrape sides of bowl and beat about three minutes.
3. Scoop into a pastry bag (or quart-sized resealable bag) with star tip.
4. Cupcakes will get a ¼ cup rosette.

VANILLA CUPCAKE

2 ¼ cups	unbleached organic flour	1 cup	rice milk
1 ¼ cups	organic sugar	1 tbsp.	apple cider vinegar
2 tsp.	baking powder	2 tsp.	vanilla extract
½ tsp.	baking soda	1 each	orange zest
½ cup	safflower oil		

1. Place all dry ingredients in mixer and mix for 2 minutes using the paddle attachment.
2. Place all wet ingredients in a separate mixing bowl and mix using a whisk.
3. Slowly add the wet ingredients, including orange zest, into mixing bowl and fold in.
4. Place cupcake liners in cupcake tin and fill each compartment leaving ¼ inch from top.
5. Bake for 16 to 18 minutes at 350°F or until toothpick comes out clean. Cool for 2 hours.

CANDIED ORANGE PEELS

2 whole	naval oranges	½ cup	organic sugar

1. Using a vegetable peeler, peel the outside skin off the oranges.
2. Slice peel as thinly as possible.
3. In a medium sized pot, boil 2 quarts of water. Place the peels in a strainer and drop the orange peels into the water and blanch for 5 seconds.
4. Immediately, remove the strainer and "shock" them into a bowl of ice water.
5. Repeat, by dropping the orange peels and removing into the ice water 2 more times.
6. After the third time, dry the orange peels out on the baking pan with clean paper towels on the bottom and top. Pat dry.
7. Place the peels in a bowl with the sugar and toss. Make sure the peels are coated with sugar.
8. Line a baking pan with parchment paper. Spread the sugar peels evenly across the sheet pan.
9. Slowly bake at 225°F for 17 to 22 minutes or until golden brown.

ASSEMBLY

1. With bottom of spoon, make a 1-inch hole in middle of each cupcake. Carefully press into body of cupcake to create a cave.
2. Fill with 1 ounce Orange Cream. Do not overflow.
3. Top with vanilla frosting. Then top frosting with 1 teaspoon chopped candied orange peels.

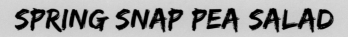

SPRING SNAP PEA SALAD

This recipe is a jump down the rabbit hole with adventurous adds like currants, blanched snap peas and orange slices. Make this your signature offering and the Queen of Artichoke Hearts will be inviting you to tea in no time.

Serves 4

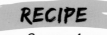

CITRUS VINAIGRETTE
Makes 2 cups

1 cup	grapefruit segments	1 tsp.	paprika
½ cup	orange juice	½ tsp.	cayenne pepper
2 tbsp.	lemon juice	1 tsp.	sea salt
2 tbsp.	lime juice	⅓ tsp.	ground black pepper
2 tbsp.	rice vinegar	¼ cup	olive oil
1 tsp.	garlic, chopped		

1. Add all the ingredients, except for oil, to a bowl and whisk for about two minutes.
2. Then begin to whisk in the oil until all ingredients are combined.

ASSEMBLY

4 cups	baby green lettuce	16 segments	orange
¼ cup	Citrus Vinaigrette	4 tbsp.	sliced almonds
1 cup	carrots, shredded	4 tbsp.	currants
16 pods	sugar snap pea, blanched		

1. In a mixing bowl, toss the lettuce with the Citrus Vinaigrette.
2. Top with shredded carrots, sugar snap peas, orange segments, almonds and currants.

132

BON VOYAGE

- Artichoke Hearts with Meyer Lemon Cream Sauce
- Orange Chicken Bites
- Summer in Asia Roll
- Curried Potato Roll
- White Gazpacho
- Shroom Burger
- Sriracha Chicken
- Kogi Slider
- Raw Salted Caramel Cheesecakes
- Raw Key Lime Parfaits
- Tart Cherry Juice with Yuzu and Vodka

It's time to celebrate again, but this time the celebration is a tad bittersweet. This menu was created for a special tribe member extraordinaire who, after 12 years with Native Foods, is embarking on a new journey abroad.

So in her honor we're partying in style, with a made-for-the-occasion menu and a toast to spontaneity, adventure and, most importantly, the friendship and love that make it all worthwhile.

We're saying *arrivederci* to those stepping into new worlds and fresh cuisines. But before our paths diverge, (we're sure they'll cross again!) we're dressing to the nines and sending our loved ones off in good taste. Use these creative courses for an unforgettable going-away bash that will make your guest of honor think twice about going away.

ARTICHOKE HEARTS WITH MEYER LEMON CREAM SAUCE

Want to bid adieu in style? Make this meal a memorable one with tempura battered artichokes and a lemon Parmesan cheese sauce.

RECIPE

Serves 18 to 20

MEYER LEMON SAUCE

⅔ cup	vegan butter	½ tsp.	ground black pepper
½ cup	Parmesan (page 71)	2 whole	Meyer lemons, zested
¼ cup	Meyer lemon juice		

1. Melt the butter in a small saucepan.
2. Stir in the cheese and lemon juice.
3. Allow the mix to cook on low heat for 3 minutes.
4. Remove from the heat and whisk in the pepper and lemon zest.

ASSEMBLY

5 each	artichoke hearts, cut into quarters	2 cups	safflower or vegetable oil
1 cup	unbleached organic flour	1 recipe	Meyer Lemon Sauce
1 recipe	Tempura Batter (page 142)	to garnish	dill, chopped
		1 pinch	sea salt

1. Cut each artichoke heart into 4 pieces. Toss the heart in the flour and dip into the batter.
2. Fry the hearts in 350°F oil for 2 minutes or until golden. Remove from the oil and tap the excess oil free.
3. Place the crisp heart in a serving spoon and top with the Meyer Lemon Sauce.
4. Garnish with fresh chopped herbs (dill would be good) and a pinch of salt.

ORANGE CHICKEN BITES

Make new friends, but keep the old. One is silver and this sweet and tangy popper is certainly gold.

RECIPE

Serves 18 to 20

MARINATED CHICKEN BITES

3 filets	meatless chicken, cut into ½-inch bite-sized pieces	2 tsp.	garlic powder
		1 tsp.	ginger powder
2 cups	unsweetened oat milk	2 cups	unbleached organic flour
1 tbsp.	sea salt	1 recipe	Tempura Batter (page 142)
½ tsp.	ground black pepper	3 cups	safflower or vegetable oil
1 tsp.	soy sauce		

1. Combine all ingredients in a bowl and marinade in the refrigerator overnight.
2. Strain the chicken bites from the marinade.
3. Toss them in the flour and dip them into the Tempura Batter.
4. Fry the bites in 350°F oil for 3 to 4 minutes or until golden.

ORANGE SAUCE

2 cups	orange marmalade	4 tsp.	sesame seeds
½ cup	pineapple juice	1 tsp.	sesame oil
½ cup	rice wine vinegar	1 tsp.	red pepper flakes
3 tbsp.	soy sauce	2 tbsp.	cornstarch
3 tbsp.	ketchup		

1. Place the ingredients together in a small saucepan and stir.
2. Bring to a boil on medium heat, stirring occasionally.
3. Once the sauce thickens, remove it from the flame and cool.

ASSEMBLY

| 1 recipe | Marinated Chicken Bites | to garnish | sesame seeds |
| 1 recipe | Orange Sauce | | |

1. Place the golden bites in a bowl and toss with the hot Orange Sauce.
2. Serve them on mini forks or skewers topped with sesame seeds.

SUMMER IN ASIA ROLL

You may not have much more time to roll with your Guest of Honor, so make sure to roll while you can with these BBQ'ed sushi bites.

RECIPE
Makes 12 rolls (cut into 6 pieces)

SUSHI RICE

2 cups	uncooked sushi grain rice	2 tbsp.	organic cane sugar
4 cups	water	1 tbsp.	safflower oil
½ cup	rice vinegar	1 tsp.	sea salt

1. Rinse the rice in cold water until the water is clear. Combine the rice with the water in a saucepan. Bring to a boil then reduce heat to low. Cover and cook for 20 minutes. It will be tender.
2. In a small saucepan, combine the rice vinegar, sugar, oil and salt. Cook over medium heat until the sugar is dissolved. Cool completely before using.
3. Pour the mix over the rice and fluff with a fork.

ASIAN BBQ'ED SEITAN

4 tbsp.	rice vinegar	¼ tsp.	Chinese Five Spice
2 tbsp.	soy sauce	1 cup	tomato paste
2 tbsp.	agave	⅔ cup	organic sugar
⅔ cup	shallots, minced	½ cup	water
4 cloves	garlic, minced	½ pound	Original Seitan (page 41), thinly sliced in ¼-inch pieces
2 tbsp.	fresh ginger, peeled and minced		

1. Stir everything except the sugar, water and seitan in a bowl.
2. In a small saucepan, slowly heat the water and sugar on medium heat. Once the sugar is dissolved, add the bowl mix to the saucepan and cook at medium heat for 5 to 8 minutes or until the sauce begins to thicken.
3. Thinly slice seitan into strips and marinate the seitan in the BBQ sauce for 12 hours.

MARINATED SHITAKE MUSHROOMS

1 tbsp.	safflower oil	4 whole	Thai chilies, soaked in hot water
2 tsp.	garlic, sliced		
2 tbsp.	ginger, minced	1 tsp.	sea salt
3 pounds	shitake caps, cleaned and stemmed	2 tsp.	agave nectar
		1 tbsp.	sesame oil
2 cups	rice wine vinegar		

1. In a saucepot, heat the safflower oil over medium heat. Add the garlic and ginger and sauté for 30 seconds. Add the mushrooms and cook for 3 minutes.
2. Deglaze the pan with the vinegar and reduce the heat until the liquid is almost gone. Add the Thai chilies, salt, agave and sesame oil and remove the pan from the heat.
3. Set the mushrooms aside and allow them to marinate for at least 4 hours in the refrigerator, if not more.

ASSEMBLY

12 whole	nori sheets	1 recipe	Marinated Shitake Mushrooms
1 recipe	sushi rice		
4 whole	avocados, thinly sliced	1 recipe	BBQ'ed Seitan
		serve with	sweet soy sauce, wasabi and ginger slices

1. Preheat oven to 350°F. Toss the nori sheets on a baking pan for 1 to 2 minutes.
2. Place the nori in the center on a sushi mat. Wet your hands and spread a thick layer of rice on the nori, leaving a ¼-inch edge clean on the top. Arrange sliced avocado on the rice. Top the avocado with the shitakes followed by 4 to 5 strips of BBQ'ed Seitan.
3. Lift the end of the mat closest to your body and gently roll the ingredients, pressing gently.
4. Roll it forward to complete the roll. Repeat with the 5 remaining nori sheets.
5. Slice each roll into 6 equal pieces and serve with sweet soy sauce, wasabi and ginger slices.

CURRIED POTATO ROLL

Distance certainly makes the heart grow fonder, but we're so taken with this sweet potato roll that we'd rather it not stray too far from our plates.

RECIPE

Makes 12 rolls (cut into 6 pieces)

CURRY MAYO

2 tbsp.	yellow curry powder	2 tsp.	garlic, minced
2 cups	vegan mayo		

1. Toast the curry powder in a dry sauté pan on high heat for 1 minute.
2. Place everything in a mixing bowl and whisk well.

PICKLED RADISHES

15 whole	radishes, trimmed and thinly sliced	2 cups	distilled white vinegar
		1 tsp.	sea salt
10 cloves	garlic	2 tbsp.	soy sauce
1 tsp.	ginger, minced	1 tsp.	organic sugar
1 tsp.	whole black peppercorn		

1. Combine the radishes, garlic, ginger and black peppercorns in a clean glass jar.
2. Add the vinegar, salt, soy and sugar. Cover and shake until the sugar and salt dissolve.
3. Refrigerate for at least 3 days, shaking once a day. These will last for 7 days in the refrigerator.

TEMPURA BATTER

2 cups	rice flour	3 cups	seltzer water
1 cup	unbleached organic flour	1 tsp.	sea salt
2 tbsp.	cornstarch		

Combine all ingredients together in a bowl and whisk well. Allow the batter to sit for at least 20 minutes before using.

TEMPURA SWEET POTATOES

2 medium	sweet potatoes	1 recipe	Tempura Batter
2 cups	unbleached organic flour	4 cups	safflower or vegetable oil

1. Slice the potatoes into ¼-inch thick slices using a food processor or mandolin. Soak in water for 5 to 10 minutes to remove excess starch. Rinse and wipe slices dry.
2. Dip the sliced potato into the flour, then dip in the batter.
3. Fry in heated 350°F oil for about 3 minutes. Remove with tongs and tap off the excess oil.

ASSEMBLY

12 whole	nori sheets	1 cup	cucumber, peeled and thinly sliced
1 recipe	Sushi Rice (page 139)		
1 recipe	Pickled Radish	1 recipe	Curry Mayo
1 recipe	Tempura Sweet Potatoes	serve with	sweet soy sauce, wasabi, ginger slices

1. Preheat the oven to 350°F. Toast the nori sheets on a sheet pan for 1 to 2 minutes.
2. Place the nori in the center of the sushi mat. Wet your hands and spread a thin layer of rice on the nori, leaving a ¼-inch edge clean on the top. Arrange 6 radishes across the rice. Top the radish with 4 to 5 slices of Tempura Sweet Potatoes and 4 pieces of cucumber. Drizzle the mayo over the potatoes.
3. Lift the end of the mat closest to your body and gently roll the ingredients, pressing gently.
4. Roll it forward to complete the roll. Repeat with the 5 remaining nori sheets.
5. Slice each roll into 6 equal pieces and serve with sweet soy sauce, wasabi and ginger slices.

WHITE GAZPACHO

With the changes of spring come other fresh starts. Embrace them with this creamy almond and fresh grape gazpacho appetizer.

RECIPE

Makes 18 to 20 shooters

GAZPACHO

1 cup	almonds, toasted	1 cup	water
4 tbsp.	pine nuts, toasted	4 slices	white bread, no crust
4 cloves	garlic, chopped	1 cup	unsweetened soy milk
5 cups	white grapes	1 tbsp.	sea salt
2 cups	white grape juice		

1. Place all ingredients in the blender and blend until smooth, about 3 minutes. You may need to do this in two batches.
2. Strain the mix into a bowl and chill for at least 1 hour before serving in 2-ounce shooter glasses.
3. Top with garnish ingredients to your liking.

GARNISH

1 whole	red grape, halved	1 pinch	chives
1 sliver	almond, toasted	drizzled	walnut oil

SHROOM BURGER

We can't imagine a better slider—one loaded with wild 'shrooms, truffle goat cheese, fresh spinach and caramelized onions. We're dancing the night away to the sound (and taste!) of this burger.

RECIPE

Makes 18 to 20 patties

SHROOM PATTY

½ pound	crimini mushrooms	2 cloves	garlic, minced
½ pound	shitake mushrooms	2 whole	shallots, minced
½ pound	bella mushrooms	2 tsp.	sea salt
½ pound	lobster mushrooms	1 tsp.	ground black pepper
½ pound	chanterelle mushrooms	2 tbsp.	fresh thyme, chopped
2 tbsp.	olive oil	1 to 1 ½ cups	panko breadcrumbs
¼ cup	vegan butter		

1. Clean each mushroom by removing the stems and brushing clean with a wet dishcloth or brush.
2. Quarter each mushroom or cut into ½-inch pieces.
3. Heat the olive oil in a pan and add the butter, garlic and shallots. Cook for 1 to 2 minutes.
4. Sauté the lobster mushrooms for 2 minutes. Then add the chanterelle, bella, shitake and crimini mushroom and cook for 2 more minutes.
5. Add the salt and pepper. Remove the sauté pan from the heat when all mushrooms are cooked.
6. Place the mushrooms in a food processor and pulse three times to break mushrooms down.
7. Place the mushroom mix in a mixing bowl and add the thyme and panko breadcrumbs.
8. Form each patty into ¼-cup portions. Line on a baking sheet and allow to cool for 30 minutes before searing.

TRUFFLE "GOAT" CHEESE

1 ½ cups	raw cashews (soaked in water overnight)	2 ½ tsp.	sea salt
		1 tbsp.	truffle oil
½ cup	safflower oil	for assembly	cheesecloth and twine
½ cup	lemon juice	1 tbsp.	cracked black pepper
2 tbsp.	tahini		

1. Place the cashews in a large bowl and cover with hot water and soak overnight.
2. After soaking, drain the liquid and rinse the nuts. Purée the cashews, oil, lemon juice, tahini, salt and truffle oil in a food processor until smooth, about 5 minutes.
3. Place a strainer over a bowl and line it with a double layer of cheesecloth. Pour the cheese mix into the cheesecloth. Twist and form the mix into a loaf and seal the ends with twine or a rubber band.
4. Set the loaf in a bowl and let it sit out at room temperature for 12 hours. Then chill for 12 hours.
5. Preheat the oven to 200°F. Line a baking sheet with parchment paper. Unwrap the cheese log and sprinkle with the black pepper. Bake for 35 minutes or until the log sets. Cool completely before crumbling.

ASSEMBLY

1 tbsp.	safflower oil	2 tbsp.	Caramelized Onions (page 85)
1 mini	vegan pretzel bread, cut in half	1 tbsp.	Truffle "Goat" Cheese
1 each	Shroom Patty	5 leaves	fresh spinach

1. Heat 1 tablespoon of safflower oil in a sauté pan and place the bun down to toast for 1 minute. Remove the bun and add the mushroom patty and cook for 2 minutes per side on medium heat.
2. Heat the onions in the pan for 1 minute per side.
3. Place the patty on the bottom half of the bun. Top with the hot onions, truffle cheese and fresh spinach leaves.

SRIRACHA CHICKEN

Shhh…the party's a surprise! Too bad these blue cheese-smothered "chicken" and crispy "bacon" sliders have us running our mouths off—they're so tasty.

RECIPE
Makes 18 to 20 sliders

MARINADE

10 filets	"chicken," cut in half	1 tsp.	paprika
2 cups	unsweetened oat milk	2 tsp.	garlic powder
1 tbsp.	sea salt	1 tsp.	onion powder
½ tsp.	ground black pepper		

Cut each filet in half. Combine all ingredients in a bowl and marinate in the refrigerator overnight.

"CHICKEN" BREADING

2 cups	unbleached organic flour	1 tsp.	black pepper
1 tsp.	sea salt	2 tsp.	garlic powder
¼ cup	nutritional yeast		

Mix all ingredients together and place in a large bowl.

SRIRACHA SAUCE

¾ cup	sriracha hot sauce	¾ cup	vegan butter

Heat the hot sauce and butter in a small pot and whisk well. Set aside.

BLUE CHEESE SPREAD

14 ounces	silken tofu, extra-firm and crumbled	2 tbsp.	apple cider vinegar
4 tbsp.	nutritional yeast	1 tsp.	garlic powder
2 tbsp.	vegan mayo	1 tsp.	ground black pepper
2 whole	lemons, juiced	½ tsp.	sea salt

Place all ingredients in a bowl and mix well. Chill for 1 hour before using.

FRIED ONIONS

1 large	white onion, thinly sliced into ¼-inch slices	⅛ tsp.	cayenne pepper
		2 cups	unbleached organic flour
2 cups	unsweetened soy milk	2 quarts	safflower oil
1 tbsp.	sea salt		

1. Place the thinly sliced onions in a bowl with the soy milk, salt and cayenne pepper and soak for about 1 hour.
2. Place flour in a separate bowl.
3. Heat oil to 375°F in a large pot or deep fryer if you have one.
4. Place a handful of the onions in the flour mixture and toss well. Tap to shake off excess flour.
5. Place onions into the hot oil and fry until golden. Remove and season with salt and pepper if needed.

ASSEMBLY

½ filet	meatless chicken, marinated	2 tbsp.	Sriracha Sauce
		2 slices	Native Bacon (page 23)
1 recipe	"Chicken" Breading		
1 whole	vegan mini bun, cut in half	2 tbsp.	Blue Cheese Spread
to fry	safflower oil	⅛ cup	Fried Onions

1. Strain the chicken from the marinade. Toss each filet in the chicken breading.
2. Heat the safflower oil in a sauté pan and place the breaded filet in. Sear until golden and crisp. Repeat on the other side.
3. Place the crisp patty in a bowl and toss with the Sriracha Sauce. Place the filet on the bottom half of the bun.
4. Heat the Native Bacon up in a hot sauté pan at medium-high heat until crisp.
5. Place the crisp bacon on top, then top with the Blue Cheese Spread and Fried Onions.

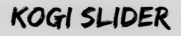

KOGI SLIDER

Here's our secret: Refuse to give your special guest this coveted recipe and they'll soon be booking a flight back into town for a "visit."

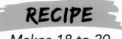

RECIPE
Makes 18 to 20

KOGI SEITAN

¼ cup	ginger, minced	½ cup	water
2 tbsp.	garlic, minced	⅛ cup	sriracha
¼ cup	organic sugar	¼ cup	sesame oil
½ cup	soy sauce	½ cup	cilantro, chopped
⅓ cup	rice wine vinegar	3 pounds	Original Seitan recipe
⅓ cup	tomato paste		(page 41), cut into
			1 x ½ -inch pieces

Place everything but the seitan in a mixing bowl and mix well. Add the seitan and marinate for 8 to 10 hours.

KIMCHI

1 head	Napa cabbage	1 cup	white onions, chopped
¼ cup	sea salt, divided	¼ cup	water
6 cloves	garlic	2 whole	green onions, minced
2 pieces	ginger (½-inch strips)	to taste	cayenne pepper

1. Cube the cabbage and wash well. Place the cabbage in a bowl and sprinkle with salt and set aside for two hours.
2. Wash and drain the cabbage. Combine the garlic, ginger and onion in the blender with the water. Blend until smooth.
3. Mix together the cabbage, onion mix, green onions, cayenne and mix well.
4. Place in airtight containers and chill for 3 days before serving.

SESAME MAYO

2 cups	vegan mayo	2 tbsp.	ginger, minced
2 cloves	garlic, minced	2 tbsp.	soy sauce
¼ cup	sesame oil	2 tbsp.	sesame seeds (black and white)

Mix everything together in a bowl and whisk well.

ASSEMBLY
Makes 1 slider

2 tbsp.	water	1 mini	vegan bun
¼ cup	Kogi Seitan	¼ cup	Kimchi, cold
1 tbsp.	Sesame Mayo		

1. Heat a small sauté pan with water. Add the Kogi Seitan with the marinade. Heat for 2 to 3 minutes or until hot.
2. Spread the mayo over one bun half and pile the hot seitan and cold kimchi. Top with other half.

RAW SALTED CARAMEL CHEESECAKES

Salted caramel creations have taken over the dessert-o-sphere. Chances are, your honored guest wants her party at the center of *that* universe.

RECIPE

Makes 16 mini cakes

SALTED CARAMEL SAUCE

1 cup	raw cashews, soaked	2 cups	Medjool dates, pitted and soaked
1 ½ cups	water	2 tsp.	sea salt

1. Soak the cashews for 4 to 6 hours then drain. Place the cashews and water in the food processor and pulse until a cream forms.
2. Add the strained dates and salt and process until smooth.

CRUST

1 cup	pecans	1 ½ cups	Medjool dates, pitted

1. Line each mini muffin pan with a mini cupcake liner.
2. In a food processor, pulse the pecans into a crumble. Add the dates and pulse until completely smooth.
3. Press 1 tablespoon of mixture firmly into each liner.

CHEESECAKE

1 cup	raw cashews, soaked	⅓ cup	Salted Caramel Sauce
1 whole	lemon, juiced		

Place all ingredients in the food processor and blend until smooth.

ASSEMBLY

1. Pour the cheesecake mix over the crust lined mini liner. Then top the cheesecake mix with the rest of the Salted Caramel Sauce.
2. Allow the mini cakes to chill for at least 4 hours but up to 24 hours before serving.

RAW KEY LIME PARFAITS

Hurry! Hurry! Don't be late!
We need you here to celebrate!
Key lime parfaits wait for you
So come and spoon a glass (or two!)

RECIPE
Makes 18 to 20 parfaits

FILLING

10 whole	avocados	¾ cup	coconut oil, melted
⅓ cup	lime juice	⅓ cup	agave nectar
2 whole	limes, zested		

Place the avocados, lime juice, zest, coconut oil and agave in the blender and blend until smooth. Set aside.

CRUST

2 cups	pecans, ground	¼ tsp.	sea salt
1 ½ cups	almonds, ground	2 tbsp.	agave nectar
6 whole	dates, pitted		

Place the pecans, almonds, dates, salt and agave in the food processor and pulse until a ball forms.

ASSEMBLY

1 recipe	Filling	to garnish	fresh fruit
1 recipe	Crust	to garnish	lime zest
to garnish	lime slices		

1. Layer each parfait glass with 1 tablespoon pecan crust on the bottom followed by 1 tablespoon of filling. Repeat for a total of 3 layers of each.
2. Garnish with lime zest, lime slices or fresh fruit.

157

TART CHERRY JUICE WITH YUZU AND VODKA

We present this Tart Cherry Juice to start your new journey with a bang! And a little buzz…

RECIPE

Serves 4

1 pound	fresh cherries, pitted (or 2 cups tart cherry juice)	1 cup	simple syrup
½ cup	water	8 ounces	vodka, chilled
½ cup	fresh yuzu juice	to garnish	organic sugar

1. If using pitted cherries, place in a blender with a little water and blend until smooth.
2. In a large pitcher, add the cherry purée (or tart juice), yuzu juice, simple syrup, chilled vodka and ice.
3. Garnish each glass with a sugar rim and pitted cherries.

To make a simple syrup, put 2 cups of sugar and 1 cup of water
in a pan on medium heat for 5 minutes. Then let cool.

Chapter Five: May

CINCO DE MAYO FIESTA

- Mexican Elote
- Baked Black Beani Zucchini Chilaquiles
- Fresh Cactus Salad
- Salsa Fresca
- Churros Chihuahua
- Horchata
- Seitan Asada
- Cinco de Mayo Sopa
- Walking Tacos
- Sabrosa Salsa Verde

When the Mexican army battled France in 1862, they probably weren't eating as well as you've been these past few months. But hardships aside, we now honor the victors (and their cherished tortillas) with an abundance of food and an all-out celebration of the red, white and green. Cinco de Mayo is now observed in epic proportions, so why not epically portion these recipes and throw your own food-frenzied fiesta?

Here's the deal, amigos: We took a lot of liberties with the recipes in this chapter. While most of them are traditional Mexican foods, some have deeper roots in Spanish or even Portuguese cuisines. But since foodies are all about meshing cultural tastes, we're sticking with these colorful dishes and rich ethnic flavors for our Cinco celebration.

MEXICAN ELOTE

There are cinco reasons why we like this elote recipe.

Uno: Did you see the teeny tiny ingredient list?

Dos: Vegan Parmesan.

Tres: No fussing with buttering your cob with this recipe.

Cuatro: The lime mayo is out-of-this-world.

Cinco: It's a totally valid excuse for pre-summer grilling.

RECIPE

Serves 5

5 whole	corn cobs, shucked	2 tbsp.	Parmesan (page 71)
2 tsp.	lime juice	½ tsp.	chili powder
2 tsp.	lime zest	½ tsp.	cumin
¼ cup	vegan mayo	¼ tsp.	sea salt

1. Grill, broil or barbeque the corn cob until tender and even on all sides, about 10 minutes.
2. Combine the lime juice, zest and mayo in a bowl.
3. Combine the Parmesan, chili powder, cumin and salt in a different bowl to makes a spicy cheese blend.
4. Once the corn is ready and hot, brush all sides with the lime mayo.
5. Then dust with the spicy cheese blend.

BAKED BLACK BEANI ZUCCHINI CHILAQUILES

*T*his traditional Mexican dish of tortilla strips, layered vegetables and black beans topped with melted cheese has us swooning, and probably romping around in a Conga line or something.

RECIPE

Serves 6 to 8

1 dozen	corn tortillas	1 tsp.	sea salt
¼ cup	olive oil	½ tsp.	ground black pepper
2 tbsp.	olive oil	1 cup	Roasted Red Peppers
1 cup	onion, finely		(page 291), chopped
	chopped	1 medium	yam, shredded
3 cloves	garlic, sliced	2 medium	zucchinis, shredded
2- 14 ½ oz cans	tomatoes, chopped	2 cups	black beans, cooked
2 whole	canned chipotle		with juice
	chilies, seeded and	2 ½ cups	vegan cheese,
	chopped		shredded (½ cheddar,
1 tbsp.	vegan adobo sauce		½ Italian)
1 tbsp.	cumin	1 cup	green onions,
2 tsp.	coriander		chopped

1. Preheat oven to 400°F.
2. Slice corn tortillas into ¾-inch strips and place in bowl and toss with the ¼ cup of olive oil.
3. Spread on a baking sheet and bake until crisp, 10 to 12 minutes.
4. In a saucepan, heat 2 tablespoons olive oil and sauté onions and garlic until lightly browned. Add tomatoes, chipotle chilies and juice, cumin, coriander, salt and pepper and let simmer for 10 minutes.
5. In a 9 x 13-inch baking dish, cover the bottom with ⅓ of the tomato sauce. Then spread out half the tortilla strips, ⅓ of the tomato sauce, shredded yam, shredded zucchini, then the black beans.

6. Pour another ⅓ of tomato sauce over the black beans, top with the rest of the tortilla strips and then the rest of the tomato sauce. Sprinkle the top with cheese.
7. Reduce heat in oven to 350°F and bake for 20 minutes, until cheese is melted.
8. Let sit to cool slightly before serving and garnish with green onions and chopped roasted peppers.

FRESH CACTUS SALAD

The "nopales," or prickly pear cactus leaves, are a main ingredient in Mexican cuisine. They have a flavor similar to green beans and peppers, with a texture almost like eggplant. But still, how bizarre is it to see "shave thorns" in recipe instructions? Ouch-ihuahua!

RECIPE

Serves 4

1 pound	fresh cactus paddles	1 cup	cooked kidney beans, drained
2 quarts	water		
½ cup	onion	½ cup	cilantro leaves, lightly chopped
3 cloves	garlic, peeled		
¼ tsp.	sea salt	¼ cup	lime juice
1 cup	corn kernels	¼ cup	olive oil
½ cup	red onion, chopped	1 tsp.	vegan adobo sauce
1 cup	pear cherry tomatoes, halved	¼ tsp.	sea salt
		1 whole	orange, zested

1. Shave thorns from cactus paddles using a vegetable peeler and cut cactus pads into thin strips (about ¼-inch wide).
2. Boil 2 quarts of water with onion, garlic and salt. Add cactus and simmer for 15 to 20 minutes. Drain and cool.
3. In the meantime, place corn kernels, chopped red onion, cherry tomato halves, kidney beans and cilantro in mixing bowl.
4. In separate small bowl whisk together lime juice, olive oil, chipotle juice, orange zest and salt.
5. Toss nopales with other ingredients and lime juice mixture.
6. Works well over lettuce leaves, garnished with fresh avocado or served with some warm corn tortillas. Serve immediately.

SALSA FRESCA

This bright and colorful classic always goes over well with guests...and over any other Mexican dish.

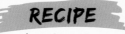

RECIPE

Makes 3 to 5 cups

2 cups	yellow and red cherry tomatoes, chopped	½ tsp.	sea salt
		1 tbsp.	jalapeños, chopped
¼ cup	red onions, diced	1 ½ cups	cucumbers, diced
1 ½ tbsp.	cilantro, chopped	¼ tsp.	cumin
1 tbsp.	lime juice		

Mix all ingredients together in a mixing bowl and let it sit for about 15 minutes.

CHURROS CHIHUAHUA

*T*hese cinnamon-sugar coated sticks of fried dough are likely of Portuguese descent, but now they're all over Mexico (and your kitchen). These "Spanish doughnuts" are slimmer and crunchier than our heavy American ones, so we're much more apt to go back for seconds.

RECIPE

Makes 40, 1-inch, 20, 2-inch pieces

CHURROS

¼ cup	safflower oil		1 tsp.	sea salt
2 cups	water		2 cups	unbleached organic flour
2 tbsp.	organic sugar		1 whole	lime, zested

1. Combine oil, water, sugar and salt in a pot on the stove and bring to a boil, stirring occasionally.
2. Remove from heat, add the flour and lime zest. Stir vigorously with a metal spoon until the mix becomes a thick, smooth ball.
3. Let the ball cool, in the pan, until it's warm enough to handle.
4. Place the mixture in a piping bag with a star-shaped tip (to make the ridges of a churro) or a Ziploc bag with the tip cut 1-inch wide. On a sheet pan, squeeze out the dough from the bag into 1 to 2 inch logs (or more depending on how long you want the churro).
5. Chill for 1 hour before frying.

CHOCOLATE DIPPING SAUCE

1 cup	vegan chocolate chips		½ cup	vegan cream cheese
⅓ cup	vegan butter			

1. While churros chill, place the chocolate chips and the butter in a double boiler for 1 to 2 minutes until melted.
2. Remove from heat and add vegan cream cheese. Set aside for dipping.

ASSEMBLY

1 recipe	Churros	for coating	cinnamon and sugar (2 tbsp. sugar with ¼ tsp. cinnamon)
1 recipe	Chocolate Dipping Sauce		

1. Fry the churros in 350°F oil in a pan until golden brown.
2. Drain on paper towels and roll in cinnamon and sugar before serving.

HORCHATA

This velvety drink of rice, cinnamon and almonds is a delicacy often sold by Mexican street vendors and dates all the way back to ancient Egypt, before it made its way to Spain and then across the ocean. It's a breeze to veganize and complements any spicy dish.

RECIPE
Serves 9

1 cup	long-grain rice	7 cups	water, divided
2 cups	almonds (no skins)	¾ cup	organic sugar
1 stick	cinnamon	for assembly	cheesecloth
1 whole	vanilla bean		

1. Grind the rice into a fine powder (a coffee grinder works well).
2. Combine the ground rice, almonds, cinnamon and seeds scraped from the vanilla bean, with 3 ½ cups of water and let it sit, covered, overnight.
3. The next day, pour the mixture into the blender and purée until smooth, adding the sugar and 2½ cups of water.
4. Strain the mixture in a strainer lined with cheesecloth. There will be a lot of solids in the cheesecloth. Be sure to press the solid to get all the liquid out!
5. Finally, add the last cup of water, whisk and enjoy.

Pronunciation guide: {or-CHAH-tah}

SEITAN ASADA

Make seitan the protein base for your burritos, quesadillas, or salads, and your guests will go loco. Cook it up "asada" style, meaning out on the grill, after you marinate it for a few hours. But be wary, this triple-threat taco topper will set your mouth aflame, so don't serve it to the faint of heart.

RECIPE
Serves 5 to 6

2 pounds	Original Seitan Recipe (page 41), cut into 1 x 1-inch slices	2 tbsp.	sea salt
		1 tbsp.	ground black pepper
		2 whole	limes, juiced
4 cloves	garlic, minced	½ tsp.	organic sugar
1 whole	jalapeño, deseeded and minced	1 cup	olive oil
		¼ cup	white vinegar
2 tbsp.	cumin	to taste	sriracha
1 cup	cilantro, finely chopped	2 tsp.	sea salt

1. Slice seitan into 1 x 1-inch slices and put into a large bowl.
2. Combine the rest of the ingredients together in a separate bowl and mix well.
3. Pour the marinade over the seitan and make sure to coat each piece well. Marinate for at least 4 hours.
4. Preheat your grill and make sure the grates are brushed with oil.
5. Remove the seitan and slightly brush off the excess marinade, but not all of it. That's the best part!
6. Place on the grill and sprinkle with sea salt. Turn the piece over after 2 minutes or so.
7. Repeat on the other side.
8. Serve with warm tortillas and sliced avocado.

Try this with our Salsa Verde on page 173

CINCO DE MAYO SOPA

*O*ur "sopa" is a take on the traditional Mexican pozole known for its hominy base. "Pozole" means foamy, which is strange because this dish hardly looks like a vegetable bubble bath. Instead, the name comes from the foam that often forms when boiling the ingredients.

RECIPE
Serves 8

¼ cup	water	1 cup	water or Vegetable Stock (page 17)
1 cup	yellow onion, diced	½ pound	Mexican Seitan (page 55)
2 cloves	garlic, minced	2 tsp.	garlic powder
¼ cup	jalapeño, diced	1 tsp.	cayenne pepper
15 oz can	kidney beans, drained	½ tsp.	chili powder
15 oz can	pinto beans, drained	2 tsp.	cumin
2 cups	hominy, plus 1 cup of the liquid	1 tsp.	dried oregano
¾ cup	green chilies	1 tsp.	onion powder
1 can	corn	1 tsp.	sea salt
2 whole	tomatoes, diced (or 1 can diced tomatoes)	1 cup	salsa of your choice
		1 handful	fresh cilantro

1. Place the ¼ cup of water in a large pot. Then add the diced onions, garlic and jalapeño. Cook for 1 minute on medium-high heat.
2. Add both beans, hominy (with juice), green chilies and corn. Cook for 7 to 8 more minutes.
3. Add the stock or water, diced tomatoes, Mexican Seitan and spices. Bring to a boil and reduce heat to a simmer. Allow the pot to simmer for 10 minutes or so to fully incorporate all the flavors.
4. Remove the pot from the heat and stir in the salsa and cilantro. Garnish with tortilla strips, cilantro, avocado or vegan sour cream to preference.

WALKING TACOS

With this holiday's vibrant dancing, you may not always have time for a table feast. Thus we present: the portable taco. Line your favorite mug with a warm tortilla and pile it high with toppings. Grab a fork—and maybe some napkins—and you're good to go. Talk about *fast* food!

RECIPE
Serves 6

¼ to ⅓ cup	olive oil	1 cup	green chilies, diced
2 cloves	garlic, chopped	2 medium	tomatoes, chopped
4 cups	pinto beans, cooked	2 cups	cabbage, chopped
½ cup	bean cooking liquid or water	2 whole	avocados, chopped
		1 ½ cups	vegan sour cream
½ tsp.	sea salt	1 cup	black olives, pitted and sliced
10 whole	corn tortillas		

1. Heat olive oil in skillet and add garlic until barely golden. Next, add one cup of the beans and part of the cooking liquid and start mashing to get proper consistency. Continue until all the beans and liquid are used. Add salt and remove from heat. Set aside

2. Heat corn tortillas on both sides by softening on griddle or skillet. Then when warm and pliable, cut them in half, then into triangles.

3. Distribute into individual cups or mugs and top with the refried beans, green chilies, tomatoes, cabbage, avocados, sour cream and black olive slices.

SABROSA SALSA VERDE

The tomatillo fruit, known as the Mexican tomato, looks like a small and delicate paper lantern, until the growing fruit inside fills the husk and splits it open at harvest. And by harvest, we mean salsa time. Serve this spicy and chunky dip with chips, enchiladas or our Seitan Asada. Que es muy caliente!

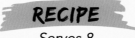
RECIPE
Serves 8

1 pound	tomatillos, husked (soak in water for 5 minutes to speed process)	1 whole	serrano pepper, chopped
½ cup	yellow onion, diced	¼ cup	cilantro, chopped with stems
4 cloves	garlic, sliced	1 tbsp.	cumin
1 whole	jalapeño pepper, chopped	1½ tsp.	sea salt
		2 cups	water

1. Place tomatillos, onion, garlic, jalapeño and serrano pepper into a saucepan. Allow tomatillos to sweat until the onions become translucent.
2. Season with the cilantro, cumin and salt. Cook for 1 more minute.
3. Add water and bring to a boil. Once at a boil, reduce heat to medium-low and simmer until tomatillos are soft, about 15 to 20 minutes.
4. Using the blender, carefully purée the mix in batches until smooth.
5. Serve over your favorite protein or with fresh tortilla chips!

MOTHER'S DAY

- Upside Down Coconut Flan
- Quickie Shallot Mushroom Quinoa Pilaf
- Asparagus Pesto Flatbread with Chardonnay Cheese
- Summer Zucchini and Tomato Soup
- Orzo Stuffed Sweet Peppers
- Arugula and Shaved Fennel with Citrus Vinaigrette
- Pear Crumble

Mother's Day is just around the corner, and if you're on the prowl for ways to spoil mom, you're in the right place, because these next bites are healthful, refreshing and bursting with spring.

But if you're on the receiving end, hoping to wake up on Mother's Day to these Native smells wafting from the kitchen, just stealthily open this book to one of your favorites and leave it on the kitchen counter. Hopefully someone will take the hint. Otherwise just flat out pre-request it. It's your day—have brunch your way.

UPSIDE DOWN COCONUT FLAN

Flan is known for its simplicity, but how do you turn it vegan? Here's the scoop: Agar flakes and kuzu give it the same custardy consistency we know and love. It's an easy fix and tastes *flan-tastic!*

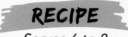

RECIPE

Serves 6 to 8

FLAN

½ cup	maple syrup		¼ cup	agar flakes
⅓ cup	cocoa powder		3 tbsp.	kuzu, dissolved in ½ cup cold water
2 tsp.	orange zest			
4 cups	coconut milk		⅓ cup	maple syrup
			1 tbsp.	coconut extract

1. In a saucepan whisk maple syrup, cocoa powder and orange zest together, then simmer until reduced to about ⅓ cup. Set aside for final drizzle.
2. In a separate saucepan, combine 4 cups of the coconut milk and agar and simmer on low until agar is dissolved.
3. Add kuzu in water, maple syrup and coconut extract and stir constantly over high heat until mixture thickens and comes to boil. Remove from heat and pour into a 9 x 13-inch pan or round, 10-inch cake pan.
4. Let set and refrigerate for two hours. Drizzle top with maple chocolate reduction.

QUICKIE SHALLOT MUSHROOM QUINOA PILAF

*T*his protein-packed side dish couldn't be tastier or more impressive considering it's an absolute quickie to make. Later you can tell Mom it required blood, sweat, and tears.

RECIPE
Serves 4

2 tbsp.	olive oil	½ tsp.	sea salt
2 whole	shallots, chopped	1¾ cups	water
½ cup	celery, chopped	1 cup	quinoa
½ pound	Portobello mushrooms, stem removed and cut in ¼-inch pieces	1 tsp.	ground black pepper

1. In a heavy saucepan heat oil and sauté shallots, celery and mushrooms with salt for 2 to 3 minutes.
2. Add water and quinoa. Bring to boil and simmer for 15 minutes until water is absorbed.
3. Add pepper and enjoy!

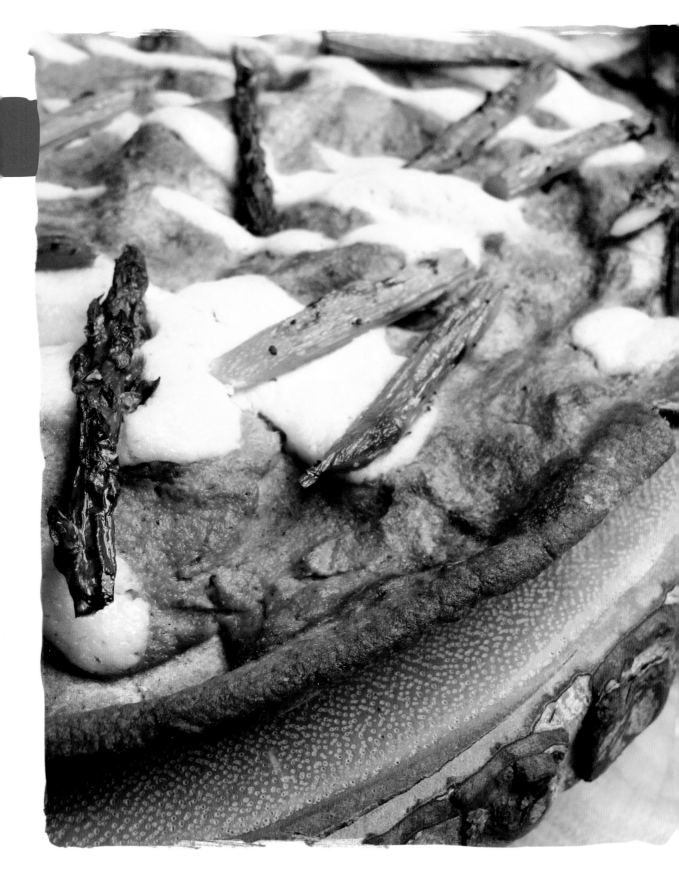

ASPARAGUS PESTO FLATBREAD WITH CHARDONNAY CHEESE

We like to think of this as grown-up pizza. Crisp lavash flatbread, roasted asparagus and dollops of homemade Chardonnay cheese mature this casual dish.

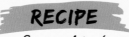

RECIPE

Serves 4 to 6

CHARDONNAY CHEESE

1 cup	cashews	¼ tsp.	sea salt
2 cups	warm water	2 tsp.	Dijon mustard
1 cup	sauerkraut	¼ cup	Chardonnay
2 tbsp.	miso		

1. Soak the cashews in 2 cups of warm water for at least 30 minutes.
2. Drain and put in blender with rest of ingredients.
3. Let sit out overnight to cultivate cultures.

ASSEMBLY

2 pounds	asparagus, grilled or roasted	2 tbsp.	pine nuts
¾ cup	olive oil	½ tsp.	sea salt
½ cup	basil	4 whole	flatbread lavash wraps
2 cloves	garlic, chopped	1 recipe	Chardonnay Cheese

1. Preheat oven to 375°F.
2. Cut tips off each grilled asparagus piece. Set aside the tips. Chop remaining asparagus and put it in a food processor with all other ingredients (except flatbread and cheese) until well blended.

3. Place whole flatbread on baking sheets, spread on asparagus-pesto mixture and bake 7 to 10 minutes until crispy.
4. Top with dollops of Chardonnay Cheese and asparagus tips. Place in oven another 2 minutes to warm.
5. Serve with more Chardonnay Cheese on the side.

SUMMER ZUCCHINI AND TOMATO SOUP

It's finally time to use that newly sprouted backyard harvest in home cooking for Ma. But, hot soup in May? You'll understand once you taste the simple garden-freshness in every slurp.

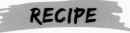

RECIPE
Serves 4 to 5

4 whole	Roma tomatoes	1 pound	zucchini
2 tbsp.	olive oil	1 tbsp.	dried tarragon
1 small	red onion, chopped	¼ to ½ tsp.	ground black pepper
2 cloves	garlic, peeled	3 ½ cups	water
1 tbsp.	sea salt		

1. Grill tomatoes until skin starts to blister.
2. Place the roasted tomatoes in blender and purée until smooth.
3. Heat olive oil in stockpot. Add onion, garlic and salt and sauté until lightly browned and translucent.
4. Add zucchini and sauté, stirring until lightly brown all over.
5. Add tarragon and black pepper and sauté another minute.
6. Add roasted tomatoes and water. Bring to a boil and then immediately turn down heat to simmer for 20 minutes.

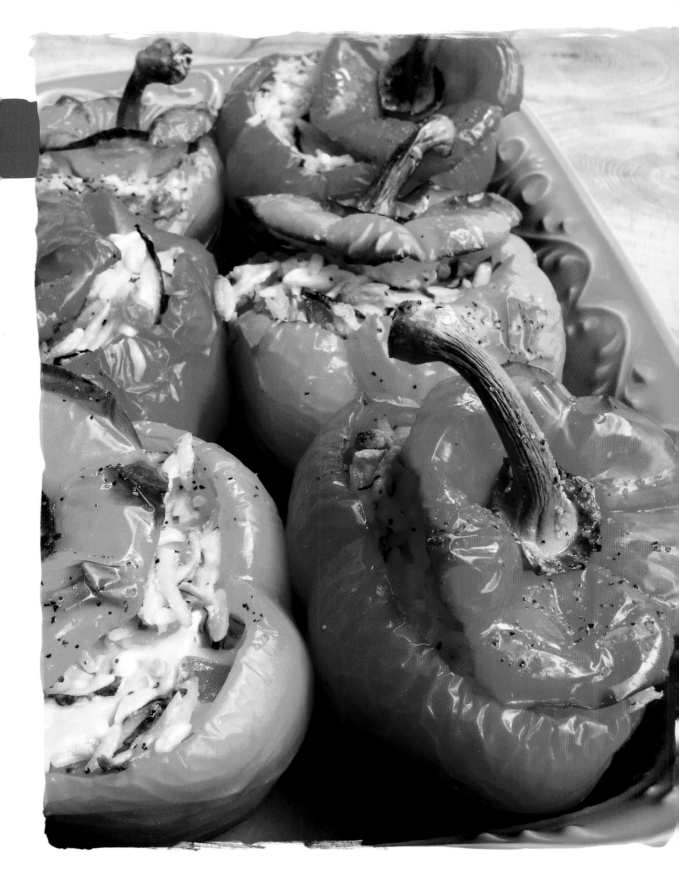

ORZO STUFFED SWEET PEPPERS

Most people do stuffed peppers with full-sized reds and yellows. But you can also use this recipe to make mini pepper poppers instead. Then voila, the plump entrée turns into an adorable appetizer that is just as photogenic.

RECIPE

Makes 6 peppers or 16 pepper poppers

1 pound	tomatoes, diced	5 cloves	garlic, minced
2 whole	zucchinis, grated	2 tsp.	garlic powder
½ cup	mint leaves, chopped	2 tsp.	sea salt
½ cup	basil leaves, chopped	2 tsp.	ground black pepper
¼ cup	vegan sour cream	6 cups	water
½ cup	vegan mozzarella cheese, shredded	2 cups	orzo
¼ cup	olive oil	6 whole	sweet peppers (or 16 mini)

1. Preheat oven to 400°F.
2. Put the tomatoes into a large bowl. Add the zucchini, mint, basil, sour cream, cheese, olive oil, garlic and garlic powder, salt and pepper. Stir to combine.
3. Bring the water to a boil in a medium saucepan over high heat. Add the orzo and cook for 4 minutes. The orzo should be only partially cooked.
4. Strain the orzo. Stir the orzo into the vegetable mix to combine. Transfer the warm water to a 3-quart baking dish.
5. Slice the tops off the peppers. On the regular sized peppers, cut a very thin slice from the base to help the peppers stand up.
6. Place the peppers in the baking dish. Scoop the orzo mixture into the peppers until full.
7. Cover the dish with foil and bake for 20 minutes. Remove the foil, sprinkle the top of each pepper with cheese and continue baking until the cheese is golden, about 10 minutes.
8. Allow to cool.

ARUGULA AND SHAVED FENNEL WITH CITRUS VINAIGRETTE

We've got this sweet spring delicacy down to a tee just for her.

RECIPE
Serves 4

CANDIED PECANS

1 cup	pecans	2 tbsp.	brown sugar
¼ cup	maple syrup	⅓ tsp.	cayenne pepper
¼ cup	agave nectar	¼ tsp.	sea salt

1. In a bowl, mix all the ingredients together well. Then in a sheet pan, line with a sheet of parchment, and pour mixture on.
2. Then bake in the oven for about 10 minutes at 350°F, stirring the mixture with a spatula every 2 minutes.
3. Remove from heat and let cool.

ASSEMBLY

1 cup	fennel, shaved	½ cup	Candied Pecans
2 whole	grapefruits, segmented	2 tbsp.	chives, chopped
1 pound	wild arugula	1 cup	Citrus Vinaigrette (page 132)
1 cup	avocado, diced		

1. To shave fennel, use a Japanese or French mandolin. If you don't have one of these, use your knife and shave it as finely as possible. Place the shavings in ice water for about 5 minutes to get them extra crunchy and then remove and place on a paper towel.
2. To cut grapefruit segments, cut the top and bottom of a grapefruit off. Then from top to bottom, shave off the rind.

3. Mix arugula and fennel together in a large bowl, then transfer to a plate or a platter and garnish with the grapefruit segments, diced avocado, pecans and chives. You can drizzle the vinaigrette on top or leave it on the side for guests to use as they wish.

PEAR CRUMBLE

In the Odyssey, Homer said pears were the "gift of the gods." So, since mothers deserve the best of the best today, (don't they always?), its pears they're after.

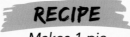
RECIPE
Makes 1 pie

FILLING

1 pound	Bartlett pears	½ tsp.	vanilla extract
½ tbsp.	brown sugar	1 tbsp.	vegan butter
½ tsp.	cinnamon	1 tbsp.	organic sugar

1. Clean pears by removing fruit from core. Slice pears ¼-inch thick.
2. In sauté pan, add pears, brown sugar, cinnamon, vanilla, butter and sugar. Cook on medium-high heat for 5 minutes. Be careful not to burn the sugars. Stir frequently.

CRUST AND CRUMBLE

1 cup	unbleached organic flour	½ tsp.	baking soda
1 cup	rolled oats	⅛ tsp.	sea salt
½ cup	brown sugar	¾ stick	vegan butter

1. Mix flour, oats, brown sugar, baking soda and salt at low speed in mixer for 2 to 3 minutes. Allow to sift together using the paddle attachment.
2. Leave mixer on low speed, add butter slowly and allow to mix. Should be a crumble, not a dough.

ASSEMBLY

1. Heat oven to 350°F.
2. Place 1¼ cups of crumble on bottom of round 9-inch pie pan. Press firmly on bottom only.
3. Evenly distribute pear mix.
4. Sprinkle remaining crumble on top of pears.
5. Bake at 350°F for 17 to 19 minutes or until golden brown on top.

EAT SUNSHINE

- Piña Colada Popsicles
- Gigi's Garden Gazpacho
- Grilled Peach with Pomegranate
- Watermelon Summer Salsa
- Grilled Mediterranean Panini on Olive Focaccia
- Rhubarb Crumble
- Cantaloupe Martini

Mother Nature has the cruel tendency to gift us the taste of summer and pull it away faster than we can lather on our SPF. Thankfully, those uncertain days are behind us and the air conditioners are upon us.

So whether you're splashing poolside or hosting a backyard affair among twinkling lightening bugs, bring your cocktail umbrellas out for a twirl and enjoy the longest days of the year. Digest the sun's rays and take a big swig out of summer with these light bites into the season's flavors.

PIÑA COLADA POPSICLES

*T*he coconut, the rum, the pineapple…might as well throw in a one-way ticket to Waikiki beach. This fun, easy-to-make dessert is the perfect treat for outdoor entertaining and transporting your guests to the tropics.

RECIPE
Serves 6

14 oz can	coconut milk	1½ tbsp.	vanilla extract
1 cup	pineapple, chopped into ½-inch pieces	2 tbsp.	rum, or ½ tsp. rum extract (optional)
1 whole	banana	1½ tbsp.	shredded coconut
3 tbsp.	agave nectar	1 cup	raspberries, for color (optional)

1. Place all ingredients in a blender (except shredded coconut and raspberries) and blend until smooth.
2. Stir in shredded coconut and raspberries (optional).
3. Pour mixture in popsicle molds and insert sticks. Or, pour into ice cube trays and insert toothpicks.
4. Freeze until solid.

Run hot water over popsicle molds for easy removal.

GIGI'S GARDEN GAZPACHO

Cool as a cucumber and blended with seasonal vegetables, this bowl of chilled goodness is bound to cool you off on the hottest of days.

RECIPE

Serves 4 to 6

4 large	tomatoes, ripe	3 cloves	garlic, minced
1 whole	hothouse cucumber, halved and seeded, but not peeled	2 ½ cups	low-sodium tomato juice
		¼ cup	red wine vinegar
		¼ cup	olive oil
2 whole	red bell peppers, cored and seeded	½ tbsp.	sea salt
		1 tsp.	black pepper, ground
1 small	red onion, diced	¼ tsp.	cayenne
1 stalk	celery, diced		

1. Roughly chop the all the veggies, except garlic.
2. In separate turns, place each veggie in food processor or blender and pulse until finely chopped.
3. Combine in a large bowl with the other ingredients. Mix well and chill.

GRILLED PEACH WITH POMEGRANATE

Veggies have always monopolized the real estate on our back patio grills, but fruits are setting up shop temporarily. Peaches warm to the grill just as easily as those peppers, and boy do they look pretty when they're done.

RECIPE

Serves 4 to 6

PESTO FETA CHEESE

1 cup	silken tofu, extra-firm and crumbled	½ cup	Basil Pesto (page 26)
½ cup	silken tofu, firm and crumbled	2 tbsp.	parsley, chopped
		1 tsp.	sea salt
3 tbsp.	lemon juice	½ tsp.	ground black pepper

1. Mix everything together in a bowl.
2. Chill for 30 to 35 minutes before serving.

POMEGRANATE GLAZE

4 cups	organic pomegranate juice	2 tbsp.	red wine vinaigrette
½ cup	brown sugar		

In a saucepot, add all the ingredients and bring to a boil. Reduce to half on medium heat. Remove from heat and let cool.

ASSEMBLY

3 to 4 medium	peaches	2 tbsp.	olive oil
½ tsp.	sea salt	½ cup	Pesto Feta Cheese
½ tsp.	black pepper, ground	2 tbsp.	Pomegranate Glaze
		½ cup	pomegranate seeds

1. Cut peaches in half and remove the pits. Sprinkle salt and pepper on peaches and drizzle with olive oil. Place on the grill for about 3 to 4 minutes until they get that nicely charred look. Remove from grill.
2. Place the feta inside the peaches. Then drizzle with pomegranate glaze and garnish with pomegranate seeds.

WATERMELON SUMMER SALSA

You know it's officially summer when the watermelon seed-spitting begins. While the kids are distracted, scoop out the pink pulp and dice it up for this vibrant summer salsa. Serve it with tortilla chips or add it to tempeh tacos for a surprising summer dinner.

RECIPE

Serves 4 to 6

3 cups	watermelon, deseeded and diced	1 to 2 whole	jalapeños, seeded and finely diced
¼ cup	red onion, finely diced	to taste	sea salt
⅓ cup	cilantro, chopped	to taste	chile con limon
2 whole	limes, juiced		

1. Mix all ingredients together (except chile con limon).
2. Chill for at least 30 minutes. When ready to serve, sprinkle with chile con limon.

GRILLED MEDITERRANEAN PANINI ON OLIVE FOCACCIA

No meat? No cheese? Then what's in it? To vegan sandwich skeptics we present this jam-packed panini as our winning defense. It's overflowing with summer lovin' and hits the spot with even the toughest critic.

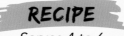

RECIPE
Serves 4 to 6

OLIVE THYME FOCACCIA

2 tsp.	dry active yeast	1 tsp.	dry thyme
1 ½ cups	warm water	1 tsp.	sea salt
1 tsp.	organic cane sugar	½ tsp.	ground black pepper
3 cups	unbleached organic flour	2 tsp.	olive oil
1 tsp.	sea salt	½ cup	Kalamata olives, pitted and chopped

1. In a large bowl, stir the yeast, warm water and sugar together. Let it sit for 10 minutes until bubbly.
2. Stir in 2 cups of flour and the salt.
3. Place the other cup of flour in a mixer and add the wet dough. Knead the dough with your hands for 3 minutes (or with a dough hook on medium speed, if you have one).
4. Transfer the dough into a large, oiled bowl. Cover the bowl with a towel and allow it to rise until it has doubled in size, about 1 hour.
5. In a small bowl, mix the thyme, salt and pepper.
6. Punch down the dough and roll it into a rectangle shape. Place it on a lightly oiled sheet pan and allow it to rise again for 30 minutes.
7. Preheat the oven to 400°F.
8. Dimple the surface of the dough with your fingertips and then brush the top surface with olive oil. Sprinkle the olives over the top, followed by the seasoning mix.
9. Bake for 17 to 20 minutes or until the edges are golden brown.

LEMON BASIL MAYO

1 clove	garlic, minced	⅛ tsp.	sea salt
2 tsp.	lemon juice	⅛ tsp.	ground black pepper
⅓ cup	fresh basil leaves, lightly packed	¾ cup	vegan mayo
2 tbsp.	olive oil	1 tbsp.	lemon zest

1. Place the garlic, lemon juice, basil, olive oil, salt and pepper in a food processer or blender until smooth.
2. Pulse in the mayo. Then stir in the zest.
3. Refrigerate before serving.

GRILLED RED PEPPER

4 large	peppers (red, yellow or green)	2 tbsp.	olive oil

1. Turn the grill onto high flame.
2. Rub the peppers with 1 tablespoon of the oil.
3. Place the peppers on the grill for 4 minutes (or until charred). Repeat on all sides until the peppers are completely charred.
4. Remove them from the grill and place them in a bowl. Immediately cover them with plastic wrap and let them sit for 30 minutes.
5. Remove the stem and the skin. Then remove the seeds from the inside of the pepper. Toss the clean peppers with the rest of the olive oil.

GRILLED EGGPLANT

2 pounds	eggplant	1 tbsp.	fresh thyme, chopped
2 tsp.	sea salt	2 tsp.	ground black pepper
4 tbsp.	olive oil		

1. Cut the eggplant into ½-inch thick round pieces.
2. Sprinkle the flesh side with salt. Allow it to sit for 30 minutes. Eggplant soaks up oil quickly.
3. Oil a baking sheet and lay the eggplant rounds down across the pan. Drizzle the top of the eggplant with the last of the oil. Place on the grill for 3 to 4 minutes. Repeat on the other side.
4. Place the grilled eggplants in a bowl with the thyme and pepper and toss well.

GRILLED GARLIC ZUCCHINI
Serves 4 to 6

1 pound	zucchini, cut into ½-inch rounds	2 tsp.	sea salt
1 tbsp.	garlic, minced	½ tsp.	ground black pepper
¼ cup	olive oil	1 tsp.	Herbes de Provence

1. Turn grill onto high flame.
2. Lightly oil a baking sheet. Lay the zucchini rounds down on the sheet pan.
3. In a small bowl, mix the garlic, oil, salt and pepper. Using a spoon or brush, cover the pieces.
4. Place the rounds on the grill for 2 minutes, then flip them over and repeat on the other side.
5. Remove them from the grill and place them in a bowl. Toss with Herbes de Provence.

ASSEMBLY

1 loaf	Olive Thyme Focaccia Bread, cut into 6 pieces, then halve.	12 pieces	Grilled Garlic Zucchini
		8 pieces	Grilled Red Pepper
½ cup	Lemon Basil Mayo	2 cups	mixed baby greens
8 pieces	Grilled Eggplant	for cooking	olive oil
		8 tbsp.	vegan butter

1. Cut each portion of focaccia bread in half. Place mayo on the top and bottom halves.
2. Layer the bottom half with Grilled Eggplant, Grilled Garlic Zucchini and Grilled Red Pepper.
3. Place ½ cup of baby greens on each sandwich on top of the veggies and put the top slice of bread on top.
4. Heat up a saucepan with the olive oil and vegan butter on medium-high heat or heat up a panini machine.
5. Place the sandwich in the pan and place a heavy soup pot or sauté pan on top for 2 minutes. Flip the sandwich over carefully and repeat on the other side.

RHUBARB CRUMBLE

If you know rhubarb's a vegetable, you're smarter than the U.S. Customs Court was back in 1947. They loved their rhubarb crumbles so much they thought rhubarb was a fruit. Identity crisis aside, we love rhubarb for it's tart flavor and high fiber.

RECIFE

Makes 2 pies

FILLING

4 cups	rhubarb, cut into 1-inch pieces	1 tsp.	vanilla extract
		½ tsp.	ground cardamom
3 cups	organic sugar	½ cup	unbleached organic flour

1. Preheat oven to 375°F. In a bowl, mix together the rhubarb, sugar, vanilla, cardamom and flour.
2. Spoon the mix into the bottom of two round 9-inch pie pans.

CRUMBLE

2 cups	unbleached organic flour	2 cups	organic brown sugar
1 tsp.	sea salt	1 cup	vegan butter, cold

1. In a food processor, pulse together 2 cups of flour, salt and brown sugar.
2. Add the butter and pulse until the pieces of butter are pea-sized. Or cut the butter into the dry mix with two forks. Spread the topping mixture over the rhubarb mixture.
3. Place the pans in the oven for 35 to 45 minutes, or until the filling is bubbly and the topping is lightly brown. Let it cool for at least 30 minutes.
4. Serve with non-dairy vanilla coconut ice cream or vegan whipped cream!

CANTALOUPE MARTINI

Pass on the wine and beer and make a drink with a little bit of an attitude. Our lush cantaloupe martini is light, refreshing and actually tastes like the fruit, but with a buzzzzzzzz.

RECIPE
Serves 1

¼ cup	watermelon, cubed	2 tbsp.	vodka
¼ cup	cantaloupe, cubed	1 tbsp.	lime juice

GARNISH

1 whole	cherry	1 whole	cantaloupe slice

1. Place the watermelon and cantaloupe in a blender and blend well.
2. Place the fruit purée and all the other ingredients in a shaker filled with ice and shake well.
3. Serve in a chilled glass. Garnish with cherries and cantaloupe slices.

GRILLIN' DAD

- Lemon Rosemary Roasted Potato Skewers
- Cheddar Broccoli Chop
- Bistro Steak Sandwich
- Chocolate Covered Cherry Milkshake Smoothie
- Roasted Corn Quickie Salad

The best way to Dad's heart is through his stomach. And after last month's Native-filled Mother's Day, he's expecting an equally inventive, incredibly delicious, totally flavorful menu made just for him. Starting to feel like a tiny grain of rice in a pressure cooker? Fear not, we've got some standout dishes up the sleeves of our chef's whites to make papa proud.

Grill together out back or let Dad put up his feet. Either way, once it's done you'll need that tin foil to pack away compliments, not leftovers.

LEMON ROSEMARY ROASTED POTATO SKEWERS

We like to shake things up at Native Foods and these skewers are anything but what you'd expect. Besides the rosemary potatoes, we've speared on some seitan sausage, corn on the cob slices, and more veggies. Dad's never seen anything like this on the grill.

RECIPE

Serves 4 to 6

MARINADE

1 cup	olive oil	2 tbsp.	fresh rosemary leaves
½ cup	lemon juice	½ tsp.	sea salt
2 cloves	garlic	¼ tsp.	ground black pepper

Blend all the ingredients in a blender or shake well in a jar.

SKEWERS

1 pound	russet potatoes, scrubbed	2 whole	red bell peppers, sliced into 1-inch squares
for assembly	bamboo skewers	1 whole	zucchini, sliced into ¼-inch half moons
1 pound	seitan sausage sliced into 1-inch pieces	2 ears	corn, cleaned and sliced in ¾-inch pieces

1. Place potatoes in a stockpot and cover with 2 inches of water. Bring to boil and then to simmer for 25 minutes so they're cooked, not mushy. Remove from water and let cool to handle.
2. Soak some bamboo skewers in hot water while potatoes are cooling to prevent them from burning on the grill.
3. Slice cooled potatoes in quarters lengthwise and then in ½-inch slices.

3. Slice cooled potatoes in quarters lengthwise and then in ½-inch slices.
4. Skewer the potatoes, seitan sausage, red bell pepper, zucchini and corn.
5. Place on baking sheet or casserole dish and drizzle with Marinade.
6. Either grill individually or bake together at 375°F, turning frequently until browned, about 15 minutes. (Caution: the marinade could "flare" up a bit and corn will "pop").

CHEDDAR BROCCOLI CHOP

Sprinkle this summer staple with tofu bacon for a layer of smoky crunch beneath this chop's sweet dressing.

RECIPE

Makes 3 cups

BROCCOLI DRESSING

¾ cup	vegan mayo	2 tbsp.	organic brown sugar
2 tbsp.	olive oil	to taste	sea salt and pepper
3 tbsp.	apple cider vinegar		

Whisk all dressing ingredients together and set aside.

ASSEMBLY

1 pound	broccoli crowns with stems, julienne stems ¼-inch thick	½ cup	carrots, shredded
		1 recipe	Broccoli Dressing
1 cup	vegan cheddar cubes	to garnish	green onions, chopped
1 cup	raisins or currants	1 pound	Native Bacon, diced
½ cup	red onions, diced		(page 23)

1. Mix cheese, broccoli, raisins, onions, bacon and carrots together. Toss in the dressing and chill for at least 30 minutes before serving.
2. Garnish with green onions.

BISTRO STEAK SANDWICH

This robust summer sandwich highlights garden tomatoes, which will be at their finest this month, and is layered with bleu cheese, arugula and fried shallots. Just one bite of this explosive combo and Dad will feel like he's on top of the world.

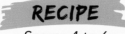

RECIPE
Serves 4 to 6

BLUE CHEESE
Makes 2 ½ cups

1 cup	vegan mayo	2 tbsp.	apple cider vinegar
2 tsp.	tahini	½ tsp.	ground black pepper
2 tsp.	garlic powder	½ tsp.	sea salt
4 tbsp.	lemon juice	14 ounces	silken tofu, crumbled

1. In a mixing bowl, whisk together mayo, tahini, garlic powder, lemon juice, vinegar, black pepper and salt.
2. Crumble the tofu into the bowl (pieces no larger than ¼ x ¼-inch) and fold into the mix.

CRISPY SHALLOTS

¾ pound	shallots	2 cups	unbleached organic flour
⅛ tsp.	sea salt	1 quart	vegetable oil (sounds like a lot, but you can save it and reuse!)
⅛ tsp.	ground black pepper		
⅛ tsp.	garlic powder		
2 cups	soy milk	1 tsp.	sea salt

1. Thinly slice the shallots and place in a bowl.
2. Add salt, pepper, garlic powder and soy milk. Soak the shallots for 2 hours and strain from liquid.
3. In batches, toss a handful of soaked shallots in a large bowl with flour. Make sure to coat the shallots well. (They should feel dry.)
4. Drop in stockpot with oil and fry for 1 to 1 ½ minutes or until golden brown. Remove using tongs or slotted spoon.
5. Place on a baking sheet lined with paper towels to remove extra oil.
6. Repeat until shallots are done.
7. Sprinkle Crispy Shallots with salt.

ROASTED TOMATOES

2 each	Roma tomatoes, quartered	⅛ tsp.	ground black pepper
		½ tbsp.	olive oil
4 cloves	garlic	4 sprigs	thyme
⅛ tsp.	sea salt	½ tbsp.	parsley, chopped

Toss all together ingredients in a casserole dish and slow roast at 325°F for 30 minutes. Remove whole thyme pieces.

STEAK SEITAN
Makes 16 ounces

½ cup	soy sauce	1 tsp.	ground black pepper
¼ cup	lemon juice	2 tsp.	garlic, minced
½ cup	olive oil	1 pound	Peppered Seitan (page 85), sliced
½ cup	water		
2 tsp.	garlic powder		

1. Place all ingredients except the Peppered Seitan in a blender and blend until smooth. Set aside.
2. Using a thin blade, slice all the thawed Peppered Seitan and place in a large baking pan.
3. Pour the marinade over the seitan and allow to marinate for at least 8 hours, no more than 12 hours.
4. Allow the seitan to drain from the marinade for 10 minutes.

ASSEMBLY
Makes 1 sandwich

1 each	French bread (6 inches), sliced lengthwise	3 each	Roasted Tomatoes
1 tbsp.	olive oil	½ cup	Crispy Shallots
½ cup	Steak Seitan	½ cup	baby arugula
½ cup	Blue Cheese	1 tsp.	parsley, chopped

1. Place French bread, sliced, in a sauté pan with 1 tablespoon of oil. Heat for 2 to 3 minutes on medium heat until golden brown.
2. Sear the Steak Seitan in a sauté pan for 2 minutes on each side.
3. On the bottom of the bread, spread ¼ cup of Blue Cheese. Place the hot seitan on top of the cheese. Then spoon ¼ cup of Blue Cheese on top of the seitan.
4. Arrange 3 pieces of Roasted Tomato on top of the Blue Cheese and ½ cup of Crispy Shallots on top of the tomatoes.
5. Place arugula on the shallots. Sprinkle with parsley.

CHOCOLATE COVERED CHERRY MILKSHAKE SMOOTHIE

Chocolate is never a bad idea. Especially when it's in the name of fatherhood and when it's providing a complete nutrition boost. "Choc" it up to the cherries and cacao powder for this antioxidant-rich shake.

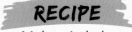

RECIPE

Makes 1 shake

1 cup	chocolate almond milk	1 tbsp.	cherry butter
1 cup	frozen cherries	1 to 2 tbsp.	cocoa powder
1 whole	frozen banana	2 tbsp.	raw cocoa nibs
1 tsp.	vanilla extract		

Place everything (except the final ingredient) in blender and blend! Pour into glass and stir in 2 tablespoons raw cacao nibs.

ROASTED CORN QUICKIE SALAD

Need a quickie? This salad is a fast and easy recipe that still packs a ton of punch. Chock full of flavor and spice, it's perfect alone or alongside beans and avocado in a tortilla.

RECIPE

Serves 4 to 6

6 cups	organic corn kernels, fresh or frozen	¼ tsp.	chili powder
		¼ cup	cilantro, chopped
2 tbsp.	olive oil	¼ cup	green onion, chopped
2 tbsp.	lime juice	¼ cup	red bell pepper, diced
1 whole	lime, zested	½ tsp.	sea salt
1 ½ tsp.	agave nectar	¼ tsp.	ground black pepper

1. If using fresh corn kernels from the cob, boil the kernels in a pot of salted water for 2 minutes and remove.
2. Heat a skillet on the stove dry—cast iron is great for this—put in corn kernels and stir while roasting, until most kernels are roasted. Let cool.
3. In a bowl toss all the ingredients together until well mixed.

STARS, STRIPES AND SLAW

- Cashew Quinoa Burger
- BBQ'ed Baked Beans
- Bread and Butter Radishes
- Citrus-Ginger Beet Slaw

Fire up the grill with your fellow countrymen and hip-hip-hooray for the good 'ole USA. Cue the sparklers, unravel the streamers, and guard your seat at the parade route. But don't forget sweet Lady Liberty's two Fourth of July musts: Fireworks and food.

From California, to the New York Island, from the Redwood Forest, to the Gulf Stream waters, we're celebrating this most important birthday with animal-friendly barbeque favorites. After all, this is the land of the *free* and the home of the brave. So let the eagles fly and the fish swim, but keep the bellies nice and full.

Our firecracker recipes are smoky, sweet, colorful and delicious. They're making Uncle Sam proud, and he wants YOU to dig in.

CASHEW QUINOA BURGER

Declare your independence from meat with this protein-packed, insanely flavorful, cashew-crunchy burger. It's so glorious you'll be signing your Hancock on the dotted line.

RECIPE
Serves 10

CASHEW QUINOA PATTY

2 cups	raw cashews	¼ cup	cumin
2 tsp.	safflower oil	2 tbsp.	coriander
2 tbsp.	garlic finely chopped	2 tbsp.	smoked hot paprika
½ cup	yellow onions, diced ⅛ inch	2 tsp.	sea salt
		2 tbsp.	tahini
½ cup	red peppers, diced ⅛ inch	1 whole	lemon, zested
¾ cup	carrots, diced ⅛ inch	¾ cup	water
2 cups	warm quinoa, cooked	7 tbsp.	wheat gluten
¼ cup	parsley, chopped		

1. Chop raw cashews in a blender for a rough chop. Do not over chop.
2. Heat oil in a sauté pan. Add garlic, onions, red peppers and carrots.
3. Cook on high flame for no more than 1 minute.
4. In a large mixing bowl, add the chopped cashews, warm quinoa, parsley, sautéed veggies, cumin, coriander, paprika, salt, tahini, lemon zest and water. Mix well.
5. Add the wheat gluten and mix well.
6. Form into patties with hands.
7. Line a sheet pan with wax paper. Place patties on pan until ready to grill.

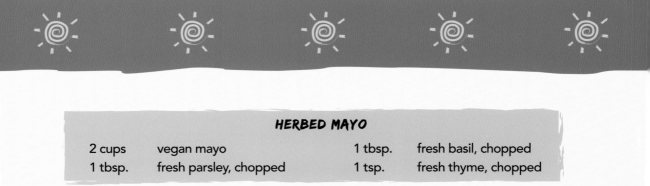

HERBED MAYO

2 cups	vegan mayo	1 tbsp.	fresh basil, chopped
1 tbsp.	fresh parsley, chopped	1 tsp.	fresh thyme, chopped

Mix everything together in a mixing bowl.

ASSEMBLY

1 whole	vegan bun, cut in half	3 tbsp.	Herbed Mayo
2 tsp.	olive oil	½ cup	romaine lettuce, shredded
1 patty	Cashew Patty	3 slices	tomato
2 tbsp.	Caramelized Onions (page 85)		

1. Brush insides of the bun with 1 teaspoon olive oil and place face-down in a hot sauté pan, until toasted.
2. Place 1 teaspoon of olive oil in the same sauté pan and place Cashew Patty down and sear for 2 minutes. Carefully flip over and sear other side.
3. Add the Caramelized Onions to the same pan for 2 minutes or until hot.
4. Spread 2 tablespoons of mayo on bottom of the bun and 1 tablespoon on the top.
5. Place the patty on the bottom bun and top with onions, romaine, and tomato slices.

BBQ'ED BAKED BEANS

Wave your vegan flag high for our version of this all-American recipe. We've taken the liberty of mixing three different kinds of beans together, instead of just one. Let freedom ring!

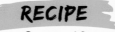

RECIPE
Serves 10

1 cup	dry pinto beans, soaked overnight	1 tbsp.	chili powder
		1 tbsp.	cumin
1 cup	dry kidney beans, soaked overnight	1 tsp.	dry mustard
		6 tbsp.	apple cider vinegar
1 cup	dry black beans, soaked overnight	4 tbsp.	molasses
		4 cups	tomatoes, diced
4 large cloves	garlic, minced	1 ½ tsp.	liquid smoke (optional)
2 cups	yellow onion, chopped	to taste	black pepper and crushed red pepper
1 tbsp.	safflower oil		
2 tsp.	sea salt		

1. Fill pot up with water until 2 inches above the beans and simmer till tender. Cook beans for 45 to 50 minutes in water while preparing the other ingredients.

2. Sauté the onions and garlic in oil for a few minutes, then add the salt, chili powder, cumin and dry mustard. Continue to cook over medium heat for 6 to 8 minutes.

3. Add the vinegar, molasses, tomatoes, liquid smoke and pepper, mixing well. Add in the cooked and drained beans and mix. Preheat the oven to 350°F. Pour the mixture into a baking dish and cover with foil.

4. Bake for 60 minutes then remove the foil and cook for another 10 to 20 minutes if you would like it thicker.

BREAD AND BUTTER RADISHES

Bread and butter radishes are a typical snack in another red, white, and blue-flagged country. (Hint: it's our baguette-loving friends). And after this recipe, we're borrowing the tradition.

RECIPE

Makes 1 small Mason jar

1 bunch	red radishes	½ tsp.	mustard seed
½ cup	vinegar, red wine or white	¼ tsp.	coriander seed, whole
¼ cup	organic sugar	½ tsp.	black peppercorns, whole
¼ cup	water	1 small	white onion, thinly sliced
2 tsp.	sea salt		

1. Rinse radishes and trim off their leafy tops (save the tops for a sauté later). Thinly slice radishes and set aside.
2. Place ingredients (except the onion and radish) in a small saucepan and bring to a simmer for about 5 to 7 minutes.
3. Remove from heat and let cool for about 5 minutes.
4. Place radishes and onions in a glass container and pour brine on top. Let sit for a half hour or so, then refrigerate. Makes a great gift packed in an old mason jar.

Perfect as a snack, veggie burger topping or
an added tangy crunch to salads.

CITRUS-GINGER BEET SLAW

Colored like the rocket's red glare, this slaw makes an excellent side dish or veggie burger topping.

RECIPE
Serves 6

¼ cup	olive oil	1 ½ lbs.	beets, peeled and julienned
2 tbsp.	red wine vinegar		
1 tbsp.	orange zest	3 whole	green onions, sliced
1 tbsp.	orange juice	½ cup	cilantro, chopped
1-inch piece	ginger, peeled and grated	to taste	sea salt and pepper

1. Whisk together oil, vinegar, zest, orange juice and ginger.
2. Toss with beets, green onions and cilantro. Sprinkle with salt and pepper to taste.

HIP, HIP, BERET!

- Seitan "Coq" au Vin
- Native 75 Mocktail
- La Quiche
- White Bean Cassoulet
- Cherry and Blueberry Clafoutis
- Beefy Bourguignon

On July 14, 1789, French commoners united in the name of liberty, equality and fraternity. Let's pay tribute by being liberal with our portions, equal in our love for each course and fraternal toward our fellow feasters.

To celebrate the resilience of another red, white and blue flag—one that flies far away in the land of crepes, croissants and excellent coffee—we've adapted some French classics for the worldly vegan palate. These recipes capture the rich, sophisticated flavors of French cuisine and will have your guests ooh-la-la-ing in no time.

SEITAN "COQ" AU VIN

*T*hough "Coq" means rooster in French, nothing in this recipe has ever cock-a-doodle-dooed. Our substitute for our farm friend is flour-dusted seitan sautéed in onions, mushrooms and garlic—soaked in vegan red wine. Bon Appétit!

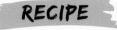

RECIPE

Serves 4 to 5

¼ cup	safflower oil, divided	1 cup	tomatoes, diced
½ pound	mushrooms, (best with a mix of oyster, button, baby bella and portobello)	2 tsp.	organic sugar
		2 cups	vegan red wine
		2 tbsp.	fresh thyme, chopped
½ cup	unbleached organic flour	1 whole	bay leaf
1 tsp.	sea salt	1 tsp.	ground black pepper
2 tbsp.	nutritional yeast	2 tsp.	sea salt
1 pound	Original Seitan, cubed or in strips (page 41)	2 cups	Vegetable Stock (page 17)
1 cup	carrots, cleaned and diced, not peeled	2 tbsp.	vegan butter
		¼ cup	water
1 cup	pearl onions (fresh and peeled, or frozen)	2 tbsp.	unbleached organic flour
4 cloves	garlic, minced		

1. Heat just 2 tablespoons of safflower oil in a large, wide pan on high heat. Sauté the mushrooms for 1 to 2 minutes only for a nice golden sear on the outside.
2. Remove mushrooms from the pan and set aside.
3. Combine the flour, salt and nutritional yeast in a bowl. Toss the seitan pieces in the flour mix.
4. Using the same sauté pan, heat the remaining oil in the pan on medium-high heat.
5. Place the dusted seitan pieces in the pan. Once they are golden brown, flip them over and repeat on the other side. Then remove them from the pan and set aside.

6. Add the carrots, pearl onions, garlic and tomatoes to the same pan. Sauté for 2 to 3 minutes. Then sprinkle with the sugar.
7. Deglaze the hot pan with the red wine. Add the chopped thyme, bay leaf, black pepper and salt.
8. Simmer on medium high-heat until the red wine is reduced by half.
9. Add the mushrooms and stock, then reduce again.
10. In a small bowl, combine the vegan butter and water until melted. Whisk in the flour.
11. Whisk the flour mix into the Seitan Au Vin to get a nice shine to the final dish.
12. Cook for 3 more minutes to ensure the flour flavor is cooked out and the sauce shines. Be sure to remove the bay leaves for serving.

NATIVE 75 MOCKTAIL

Many a glass will be raised today, so why not fill yours with this citrus-y refreshment? It's plenty tasty without alcohol, but we recommend adding orange bitters. Just remember to make eye contact during a toast, or your French comrades will think you awfully rude.

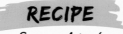

RECIPE

Serves 4 to 6

3 tsp.	organic sugar	1 bottle	champagne, chilled
12 dashes	orange bitters	6 whole	lemon wedges
6 fluid oz	ginger ale or gin	6 whole	orange twists

1. Mix the first 4 ingredients together gently so carbonation does not disappear, then portion into glasses.
2. Float a lemon wedge and an orange twist in each glass.

LA QUICHE

This petite pie will forever be a mainstay in Parisian cafés and in our hearts.

RECIPE

Serves 6 to 8

CRUST

¼ cup	millet		¾ tsp.	sea salt
1 ½ cups	flour (unbleached or whole wheat pastry)		⅓ cup	cold water
			⅓ cup	olive oil
½ tsp.	baking powder			

1. Preheat oven to 350°F

2. Toast the millet by putting it in a skillet and heat over a medium flame, stirring or shaking until millet starts to brown and slightly pop. Remove from heat and let cool.

3. In a mixing bowl combine toasted millet, flour, baking powder and salt. Add water and oil and mix well with a spoon until mixture becomes a dough. Wrap it in plastic and store in refrigerator while you make the filling.

FILLING

½ cup	water		3 tbsp.	olive oil
½ cup	cashews		2 whole	shallots, finely chopped
14 ounces	silken tofu, firm		2 cloves	garlic, thinly sliced
3 tbsp.	nutritional yeast		½ pound	mushrooms, thinly sliced
2 tbsp.	Dijon mustard		1 tbsp.	balsamic vinegar
2 tbsp.	lemon juice		2 tbsp.	olive oil
1 ½ tsp.	sea salt		2 slices	Native Bacon (page 23)
4 leaves	red chard		1 tsp.	paprika

In Paris, during 1997, Chef Marcotullio completed the world's largest quiche Lorraine. It measured 16 feet wide.

1. Combine water, cashews, silken tofu, nutritional yeast, Dijon mustard, lemon juice and salt in a blender until smooth and transfer to a mixing bowl.
2. Drain water from firm tofu and using hands, crumble tofu finely into blended tofu mixture.
3. Prepare chard leaves by cutting out stem from the green leafy part. Cut the stems in ¼-inch slices on a bias.
4. Chop the chard leaves in ½-inch pieces.
5. Heat the olive oil in a skillet and add the shallots, garlic and chard stems. Sauté until shallots get translucent, then add mushrooms and sauté another 2 to 3 minutes until they are lightly browned.
6. At end of sauté, add balsamic vinegar to remove particles and flavor off bottom of pan. Put chard-mushroom mixture into tofu mixture and mix well.
7. In another skillet heat 2 tablespoons of olive oil. When hot, add Native Bacon slices. Sauté until both sides are brown and slightly crispy.
8. Cut into ¼-inch slices and fold into tofu filling.
9. In a 10-inch pie tin or fluted quiche baking dish, place crust dough in center. Push and spread to fit bottom of pie tin, using the plastic wrap beneath your fingers.
10. Pour filling into crust, sprinkle top with paprika and bake for 50 to 60 minutes. If you can find a sweet Spanish smoked paprika, this adds a nice touch, but use sparingly—it has a kick!

WHITE BEAN CASSOULET

"Cassoulet" is the classy French twist on our word, "casserole." So we've created a dish—with white beans, thyme and parsnip—that's just as refined.

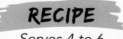
RECIPE
Serves 4 to 6

2 cups	water or Vegetable Stock (page 17)		1 medium	celery root, peeled and diced
1 cup	yellow onion, diced		2 whole	bay leaves
5 cloves	garlic, minced		3 tbsp.	fresh thyme, chopped
1 cup	carrots, cleaned and diced, not peeled		1 cup	tomatoes, diced
			3 tbsp.	tomato paste
2 whole	parsnips, peeled and diced		2 cups	cooked white beans
			1 tsp.	ground black pepper
1 stalk	celery, diced		1 tsp.	sea salt
			2 tsp.	garlic powder

1. In a large soup pot, place ⅓ cup of stock or water and sauté the onions and garlic until translucent, about one minute.
2. Add the carrots, parsnips and celery root and cook for 2 more minutes.
3. Add the celery and the rest of the broth and bring to a boil.
4. Once boiling, reduce the flame to medium and add the bay leaves, fresh thyme, diced tomatoes, and tomato paste, stirring well.
5. Cook for another 5 to 6 minutes, or until the celery root and parsnips are tender to the bits.
6. Add the beans, pepper, salt and garlic powder.
7. Cook for another 5 minutes then remove the bay leaf.

CHERRY AND BLUEBERRY CLAFOUTIS

The clafoutis is a baked French dessert, typically filled with cherries and a flan-like batter. In our version we have not one, but two super fruits storming the Bastille armed with vitamins, iron, and fiber.

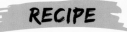

RECIPE

Makes 9 pieces

CINNAMON CREAM

14 oz	silken tofu		¼ cup	agave nectar
3 tbsp.	non-dairy milk		1 tsp.	ground cinnamon

Place all goodies in the blender and blend until smooth.

CLAFOUTIS

½ cup	unbleached organic flour, or whole wheat pastry flour		1 tsp.	vanilla extract
			¼ cup	non-dairy milk
			1 cup	blueberries
1 tbsp.	organic cornstarch		1 cup	cherries, tart and pitted
14 ounces	silken tofu		½ cup	organic sugar

1. Preheat oven to 375°F.
2. Whisk together the flour and cornstarch in a bowl.
3. Place the tofu, vanilla, half of the non-dairy milk and sugar in the blender. Blend until smooth.
4. Slowly add the tofu cream to the flour bowl. Then add the other half of the milk.

Having trouble getting this dessert's name off your tongue?
The French pronounce it "klafuti."

5. Using a spatula, fold in the blueberries and cherries.
6. Lightly grease a pie pan or small glass cake pan with pan spray or safflower oil.
7. Pour the batter into the pan and bake for 40 to 45 minutes.
8. Serve warm with a scoop of Cinnamon Cream.

BEEFY BOURGUIGNON

This onetime "peasant dish" is now a trademark of haute French cuisine. To make ours an equally respected culinary art, we "beefed" up the recipe with an array of vegetables, seasoned seitan, and plenty of wine.

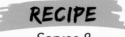
RECIPE
Serves 8

⅓ cup	olive oil	2 tbsp.	unbleached all-purpose flour
1 large	carrot, peeled and diced	2 cups	dry red wine
1 cup	yellow onion, diced	3 cups	water
1 pound	frozen pearl onions	2 cubes	vegan vegetable bouillon
1 pound	button mushrooms, cleaned and quartered	1 tbsp.	tomato paste
2 cloves	garlic, finely chopped	½ tsp.	dried thyme
1 tsp.	sea salt	1 whole	bay leaf
¼ tsp.	ground black pepper	1 cup	Italian parsley, chopped
3 pounds	Original Seitan (page 41), cut in ½-inch pieces		

1. In a large stockpot heat olive oil, carrot , onions, mushrooms, garlic, salt and pepper and sauté until transparent and lightly browned.
2. Add the seitan pieces for about 2 minutes, stirring frequently.
3. Add the flour and stir well to cover all ingredients and lightly brown, about 2 to 3 minutes.
4. Stir in wine and water. Crumble and add bouillon cubes, tomato paste, thyme and bay leaf.
5. Let simmer on low, partially covered for 1 hour.
6. Remove bay leaves and fold in chopped parsley. Serve over noodles, boiled new potatoes, or green salad and, of course, with a glass of red wine.

LAST DAY AT THE BEACH

- Way Hip Muhammara Dip
- BLTease
- 7 Layer Greek Salad
- Chik'n Picnic'n Salad
- Drunken Tofu Banh Mi

With the final days of summer looming large, take advantage of the work-hard-play-harder season before it's back to the autumn grind. Gather your crew and spend a lazy weekend sinking your toes into the sand. We can picture it now. Canopies line the beach, buckets and shovels dot the shore, and the salt mixes into your hair. But there's something missing.

Grub. After the Frisbee's been tossed and the sandcastle built, it's time for beach-inspired recipes and a break from the heat. Our portable dishes make for a worry-free meal that you can tote in one armful (at most) to the shore. Oh, and don't leave behind the bottle opener—forgetting that is no day at the beach.

WAY HIP MUHAMMARA DIP

Cool off in the surf after dipping into this spiced red pepper dip. It's perfectly portable and tasty whether it's warm or chilled. Pair it alongside pita wedges and veggies for a mid-day snack.

RECIPE

Serves 6

⅔ cup	walnut pieces, roasted and lightly ground	4 tsp.	pomegranate molasses (specialty stores)
1 pound	Roasted Red Peppers (page 291)	2 tsp.	cumin
1 ¼ cups	whole wheat breadcrumbs	1 tsp.	sea salt
6 cloves	garlic, sliced	1 tsp.	crushed red pepper
2 tbsp.	lemon juice	½ cup	olive oil

1. Toast the walnuts, either in a pan or in the oven at 350°F. Be very careful not to burn the walnuts! As soon as you can start to smell them, they are definitely done. Place them in a food processor or a blender and grind them up slightly to smaller pieces.
2. Put the roasted peppers, bread crumbs, garlic, lemon juice, pomegranate molasses, cumin, salt and crushed red pepper in a food processor and blend until smooth. You may need to process in two batches.
3. On low speed, gradually add the olive oil.
4. Pour mixture into the bowl with the ground walnuts and stir until well blended.

BLTEASE

Think you know how to build a sandwich? How about this sandcastle-tall masterpiece stacked with smoky tofu bacon, tomato and avocado? Give it a try, then squeeze it into a to-go container to join you in the sand.

RECIPE

Sweet-n-Savory Bacon
Makes 1 Tease and extra Tofu Bacon

¼ cup	water		¼ tsp.	garlic powder
2 tbsp.	soy sauce		¼ tsp.	onion powder
2 tbsp.	maple syrup		¼ tsp.	smoked paprika
½ tsp.	liquid smoke		1 tbsp.	rice vinegar
½ tsp.	mirin wine		1 tbsp.	nutritional yeast
¼ tsp.	ground black pepper		7 ounces	tofu, firm and sliced in ⅛-inch-wide slices

1. Add all ingredients except for the tofu in a bowl and mix until fully incorporated.
2. Marinate tofu for 6-8 hours.
3. Pat dry and place on parchment paper on baking sheet.
4. Bake at 400°F for 30 minutes until crisp.

ASSEMBLY

2 slices	sandwich bread		¼ each	avocado
1 tbsp.	vegan mayo		2 slices	Sweet-n-Savory Bacon
2 slices	tomato		½ tsp.	parsley, chopped
1 leaf	lettuce		1 tbsp.	red peppers, diced
2 to 3 rings	red onion			

244

1. Grill bread lightly on both sides. Spread ½ tablespoon of mayo on each slice.
2. Add tomatoes, lettuce and red onion to your liking and top with avocado.
3. Cut bacon slices in half and place side-by-side on top of the avocado.
4. Garnish with parsley and diced red pepper on top.

7-LAYER GREEK SALAD

We're ogling over this Mason jar creation of feta "cheese," Kalamata olives and a host of other flavorful veggies. Throw this refreshing favorite in your beach bag for lunch on the go.

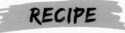

RECIPE

Serves 6 to 8

GREEK DRESSING

4 cloves	garlic, minced	1 tsp.	sea salt
3 tbsp.	fresh oregano, chopped	½ tsp.	ground black pepper
½ tsp.	Dijon mustard	½ cup	olive oil
¼ cup	red wine vinegar	1 tbsp.	fresh mint, chopped

Place all ingredients in a mixing bowl and whisk together well. Set aside.

FETA CHEESE

¼ cup	olive oil	2 tbsp.	fresh basil, chopped
¼ cup	water	½ tsp.	fresh oregano
½ cup	red wine vinegar	½ tsp.	ground black pepper
2 tsp.	sea salt	1 pound	silken tofu, firm

1. Cube the tofu into ½ x ½-inch cubes.
2. Place in a bowl and add all the other ingredients. Mix well and allow it to sit at room temperature for at least an hour.

ASSEMBLY

1 whole	Roasted Red Pepper (page 291)		½ cup	chickpeas
1 recipe	Feta Cheese		⅔ cup	artichoke hearts, quartered
⅔ cup	Kalamata olives, halved		1 cup	heirloom cherry tomatoes, halved
1 whole	Persian cucumber, sliced in ¼-inch pieces		1 recipe	Greek Dressing
1 whole	yellow pepper, roasted			

1. Julienne your roasted pepper.
2. Remove the Feta Cheese from the marinade.
3. Layer each jar with the vegetables, chickpeas and cheese. Make sure to have the feta in the middle of the jar. Pour the dressing over the top and seal the lid. Refrigerate for a total of 24 hours. Flip the jar over every 4 hours, or at least 4 times.

CHIK'N PICNIC'N SALAD

Vegans have a major advantage when it comes to picnic food. Our "mayo" doesn't spoil nearly as fast in the heat. So for your beach day bash, bring on the chick'n salad even under the sun's rays.

RECIPE
Serves 4

2 tbsp.	olive oil	4 tbsp.	vegan mayo
8 ounces	meatless chicken strips	¾ tsp.	Dijon mustard
1 stalk	celery, chopped into ¼-inch pieces	½ tsp.	lemon juice
		½ tsp.	hot sauce
1 small	carrot, chopped into ¼-inch pieces	¼ tsp.	sea salt
		⅛ tsp.	ground black pepper
½ cup	onion, finely chopped		

1. Heat olive oil in skillet on medium heat and add Chicken-less Strips.
2. Sauté until lightly browned about 3 to 4 minutes, then let cool.
3. Chop Chicken-less Strips into ¼-inch to ½-inch pieces and place in mixing bowl.
4. Add rest of ingredients and mix together well.

DRUNKEN TOFU BANH MI

Stuffed with crispy tofu in a sweet chili marinade, this tangy sandwich monstrosity will have you licking your fingers clean.

RECIPE

Serves 5 to 6

DRUNKEN TOFU MARINADE
Makes 3 cups

4 medium	shallots, sliced	2 cups	rice vinegar
2 whole	lemongrass, 2-inches long, smashed	½ cup	sweet chili sauce
		4 tsp.	organic sugar
3 cloves	garlic, whole		

Place all ingredients into the blender and blend until smooth.

DRUNKEN TOFU

2- 14 oz boxes	silken tofu, firm	1 recipe	Drunken Tofu Marinade
1 quart	vegetable oil		

1. Cut the tofu blocks into 24 pieces.
2. Fry tofu in a soup pot with oil at 350°F for 4 minutes or until golden brown and crispy. You will need to do this in separate batches. Allow the tofu to drain for 1 minute.
3. Place the tofu steaks into a casserole dish and cover with the Drunken Tofu Marinade.
4. Allow the tofu to marinate for 12 to 16 hours maximum.

DRUNKEN TOFU SAUCE

2 tbsp.	ginger, minced	¼ cup	safflower oil
4 cloves	garlic, whole	⅓ cup	sriracha
¼ cup	soy sauce	¼ cup	agave syrup
¼ cup	lime juice	¼ cup	water

Place all the ingredients into the blender and blend until smooth.

KIMCHI SLAW DRESSING

1 tsp.	chili powder	2 tbsp.	ginger, minced
4 cloves	garlic	½ cup	soy sauce
¼ cup	green onions, chopped	¾ cup	rice vinegar

Place all ingredients in the blender and blend until smooth.

KIMCHI SLAW

3 cups	cabbage, shredded	1 cup	green onion, chopped
2 cups	carrots, shredded	⅓ cup	Kimchi Dressing
1 cup	red onion, sliced in ¼-inch half moons		

1. In a large bowl toss the cabbage, carrots and onions together.
2. Add the Kimchi Dressing and toss again. Mix well.

PICKLED JALAPEÑOS

2 tbsp.	sea salt	¼ tsp.	oregano
2 quarts	water	1 tsp.	cumin
1 pound	jalapeños	1 ½ tbsp.	garlic, finely chopped
½ cup	safflower oil	¾ tsp.	sea salt
½ cup	apple cider vinegar		

1. Mix salt and water together in large bowl.
2. Remove the top and stem from the jalapeños using protective gloves. Slice lengthwise into ¼-inch slices. Using a mandolin, slice the jalapeños directly into salt water to stop heat.
3. Let sit and brine for 12 hours.
4. After 12 hours, mix the rest of the ingredients together in a bowl and pour over jalapeños. Let marinade for minimum of 1 hour. These should last refrigerated for 3 days.

PICKLED CARROTS AND DAIKON

2 cups	warm water	2 tbsp.	sea salt
¼ cup	apple cider vinegar	1 whole	carrot
¼ cup	agave nectar	½ pound	daikon

1. Combine warm water, vinegar, agave and salt in a mixing bowl.
2. Peel carrots and daikon.
3. Using the shredding attachment on the food processor, shred the carrots and daikon separately, then combine.
4. Cover with vinegar mixture. Let chill and marinade for a minimum of 30 minutes

ASSEMBLY

1 each	French baguette	⅓ cup	Drunken Tofu Sauce
1 block	Drunken Tofu Steak	2 leaves	fresh basil
¼ cup	Caramelized Onions (page 85)	6 sprigs	fresh cilantro
		1 cup	Kimchi Slaw
¼ cup	Pickled carrots and Daikon	1 tsp.	toasted sesame seeds
2 tbsp.	Picked Jalapeño	1 sprig	fresh cilantro

1. Brush the grill or flat top with oil and toast the baguette until golden brown inside.
2. Brush the flat top again with oil and sear Drunken Tofu pieces for 1 ½ minutes. Flip and repeat on the other side.
3. Reheat the onions in a hot sauté pan for 1 ½ minutes per side.
4. Layer the 5 slices of tofu on the bottom part of the baguette.
5. Squeeze the Drunken Tofu Sauce over the tofu.
6. Place the hot onions on the tofu then layer the other ingredients (pickled daikon and carrots, pickled jalapeño, whole basil and whole cilantro).
7. Serve the Kimchi Slaw on the side.
8. Garnish slaw with toasted sesame seeds and a sprig of cilantro.

SEASON'S BERRY BEST

- Lavender Panna Cotta with Fresh Berries & Almond Cookie Crumble
- Raspberry Beret Smoothie
- Four Simple Blueberry Pancakes
- Blueberry Strawberry Crumble
- Blueberry Lemon Bars
- Strawberry Shortcake with Almond Crème

From aronia berries and barberries to olallieberries and yumberries, produce aisles across the U.S. are learning a whole new alphabet of tiny fruit. With consumer demand skyrocketing and new varieties being cultivated every season, it can be hard to keep up with exactly what berry is what. So for old times' sake, we'll stick to our familiar friends: blueberry, strawberry and raspberry.

These sweet delights are extra plump in August, when they become so saturated with color that we're eating them right off the bush.

Whether you've just returned from a family picking trip, or grabbed a box at your local farmer's market, use these treats in sweet recipes before they soften (unless, of course, you plan on popping them by the fistful until you've emptied the box).

LAVENDER PANNA COTTA WITH FRESH BERRIES & ALMOND COOKIE CRUMBLE

Use whatever seasonal berry suits your fancy for this high-brow dessert. Panna Cotta is a classic Italian custard, but we make ours dairy-free with soy yogurt and agave. Are you drooling yet?

RECIPE

Serves 4 to 6

PANNA COTTA

2 tbsp.	dried lavender		¼ cup	agave nectar
1 ½ cups	soy milk		1 ½ cups	vanilla soy yogurt
4 tbsp.	agar agar			

1. Steep the dried lavender in the soy milk, in a saucepan on medium-low heat, for 5 to 7 minutes.
2. Strain the soy milk and return it to the flame. Add the agar agar and agave and bring to a slow boil. The agar agar must dissolve.
3. Remove from the heat and whisk in the yogurt.
4. Portion into mold or dishes of your desire and cool for 3 to 4 hours.

CARAMEL SAUCE

2 cups	organic sugar		½ cup	coconut milk
¼ cup	agave		2 tbsp.	vegan butter
½ cup	water		1 pinch	sea salt

1. In a small saucepan over medium-high heat, bring the sugar, agave and water to a boil, stirring well to dissolve the sugar.
2. Turn down the heat to low and cook until the liquid is deep amber in color, about 12 minutes, moving the pan around occasionally to ensure even cooking.
3. Remove the pan from heat. Very carefully (the mixture will bubble), stir in the coconut milk, dairy-free margarine and salt until smooth.

ALMOND COOKIES
Makes 10 cookies

½ cup	almond butter		1 tsp.	vanilla extract
2 cups	almond flour meal		to garnish	almonds, sliver
6 tbsp.	agave nectar			

1. Preheat the oven to 350°F.
2. Place all the ingredients in a bowl and stir to thoroughly combine.
3. Roll the dough into 1-inch balls and lightly press down with a fork or your fingers.
4. Place the cookies on a lined baking sheet.
5. Bake 10 to 12 minutes or until golden. The cookies will crisp as they cool. Then crumble.

ASSEMBLY

Before serving, drizzle cooled Panna Cotta with Caramel Sauce. Scatter crumbled Almond Cookies and mixed berries over the top.

RASPBERRY BERET SMOOTHIE

Whether you need a poolside refreshment or a post-run pick-me-up, this cold, nutrient-rich beverage full of dietary fiber and Vitamin C will do the trick.

RECIPE
Serves 2

2 cups	coconut milk	2 tbsp.	hemp seeds
1 cup	fresh organic raspberries	¼ tsp.	ground cinnamon
½ cup	ice	2 tbsp.	maple syrup
2 tbsp.	water		

Place all ingredients in the blender and blend until smooth.

FOUR SIMPLE BLUEBERRY PANCAKES

A steaming short stack is just the thing for a lazy Sunday morning, and berries look great between the folds. So start your day on the right foot and be sure to double (or triple) the recipe if you're feeding the whole gang.

RECITE
Serves 4

1 cup	unbleached organic flour		⅛ tsp.	sea salt
3 tbsp.	sugar or 1 ½ tbsp. agave nectar		1 cup	almond milk
1 tbsp.	baking powder		1 cup	blueberries

1. Whisk together flour, sugar, baking powder and salt in large bowl. Slowly whisk in almond milk.
2. Heat a non-stick pan over medium heat. Pour ¼-cup batter into hot pan and dot with blueberries. Cook 3 to 4 minutes or until batter begins to bubble and pancake edges start to brown.
3. Flip and cook 2 to 3 minutes more, or until cooked through and golden on both sides. Repeat until all pancakes are made. Store in a warm oven while finishing the rest.

BLUEBERRY STRAWBERRY CRUMBLE

*T*he magic of the blueberry is that it's sweet all by itself but still plays well with others. That's why we pair it with strawberries in this crumble recipe. Around-the-house ingredients like cornstarch and oats make it a perfectly spontaneous treat for your neighbor next door.

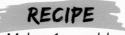

RECIPE
Makes 1 crumble

FILLING

1 ½ cups	frozen blueberries, thawed and drained	1 tbsp.	lemon juice
		⅓ cup	organic sugar
1 ½ cups	organic strawberries, cut into ¼-inch slices	3 tbsp.	cornstarch

1. In a saucepan, add the blueberries, strawberries, lemon juice and sugar. Cook on medium heat until the sugar is well mixed and the berries are tender, about 4 to 6 minutes.
2. Turn the heat down to low and stir in the cornstarch, 1 tablespoon at a time. Bring the heat back up to medium and allow the berry mix to come to a boil.
3. Once the mix boils, it will start to thicken. Remove it from the heat and set aside.

CRUMBLE

1 cup	unbleached organic flour	⅓ tsp.	baking soda
1 cup	oats	1 pinch	sea salt
⅔ cup	brown sugar	½ cup	vegan butter, soft

1. Mix the flour, oats, brown sugar, baking soda and salt on low speed in the mixer for 2 to 3 minutes. Use the paddle attachment.
2. Leave the mixer speed on low, then slowly add the butter and allow it to mix until it forms a crumble—not a dough.

ASSEMBLY

½ tsp.	vegan butter	1 recipe	Crumble
2 tbsp.	unbleached organic flour	1 recipe	Filling

1. Heat oven to 350°F.
2. Grease the bottom of a pie shell with ½ teaspoon of butter and 2 tablespoons of flour.
3. Press crumble firmly on the bottom of the pie shell. This crust does not need to be pressed up the sides of the pan.
4. Evenly distribute the berry mixture on the bottom of the pan.
5. Take the remaining crumble and sprinkle on top of the berry mix.
6. Bake at 350°F for 30 to 35 minutes or until golden brown on top and the berries bubble on the side.
7. Allow the pie to cool completely before serving.

BLUEBERRY LEMON BARS

Blueberry and lemon meet for a clandestine rendezvous in these pretty-as-a-picture dessert bars. Garnish them with a swirl of blueberry and agave glaze and watch the jaws drop.

RECIPE

Makes 16 bars

BLUEBERRY GLAZE

4 cups	frozen blueberries	1 cup	agave nectar

1. Defrost blueberries completely.
2. Place in blender with agave and blend until completely mixed and puréed.

CRUST

15 ounces	vegan margarine	4 cups	unbleached organic flour
¾ cup	powdered sugar		

1. Place margarine and powdered sugar in the mixer and mix on low speed for 3 minutes or until well incorporated.
2. Slowly add in the flour and mix for another 30 to 40 seconds until the dough forms a ball.
3. Spread the dough evenly across the half-sheet pan.
4. Bake at 250°F for 14 to 16 minutes until crust is lightly golden. Allow to cool completely.

FILLING

14 ounces	silken tofu, firm	⅔ cup	unbleached organic flour
3 ¾ cups	organic sugar	⅔ cup	cornstarch
6 whole	lemons, zested	8 ounces	Blueberry Glaze
1 ¾ cups	lemon juice		

1. Place the tofu, sugar, lemon zest, lemon juice and flour into the blender. Blend until smooth. Make sure to scrape the sides.
2. Add the cornstarch and blend for 30 more seconds.
3. Pour the mix over the cooled cookie dough.
4. Using a fork, zigzag the Blueberry Glaze across the lemon mix, leaving very little yellow color.
5. Bake at 350°F for 20 to 22 minutes or until the mix has almost set. (The middle may move a bit—it's alright.)
6. Allow the pan to cool completely before serving. The middle will firm up.

STRAWBERRY SHORTCAKE WITH ALMOND CRÈME

When it comes to flavor, this cake is anything but short. Our moist vanilla cake absorbs the drips and drops of fresh strawberries and almond crème, all while standing perfectly tall.

RECIPE

SHORTCAKE

2 ¼ cups	unbleached organic flour	½ cup	safflower oil
1 ¼ cups	organic sugar	1 ½ cups	rice milk
2 tsp.	baking powder	1 tbsp.	apple cider vinegar
½ tsp.	baking soda	2 tsp.	vanilla extract
½ tsp.	sea salt		

1. Sift all dry ingredients together and place in a mixing bowl.
2. Whisk and create a "well" for the wet ingredients.
3. Place all the wet ingredients in a separate mixing bowl and mix using a whisk.
4. Slowly add the wet ingredients into the mixing bowl and fold in.
5. Place cupcake liners in the cupcake tin, and fill each compartment leaving ¼ inch from the top.
6. Bake for 15 to 18 minutes at 325°F, or until a toothpick comes clean. Cool for 2 hours.

STRAWBERRY SHORTCAKE CRÈME

¾ pounds	vegan cream cheese	¾ cup	soy milk
2- 14 oz boxes	silken tofu, extra-firm	1 tsp.	almond extract
½ cup	agave nectar		

Place all ingredients in a bowl and, using a hand-mixer, mix until smooth. Cool.

ASSEMBLY

1 recipe	Shortcake	2 whole	fresh strawberries, cut in ⅛-inch pieces
⅓ cup	Strawberry Shortcake Crème		

1. Cut the cupcake in half. Place the bottom in a 9 ounce clear glass.
2. Ladle ¼ cup of the crème in the cupcake. Lay out one sliced strawberry against the side of the cup.
3. Place the top half of the cupcake on top of the crème, leaving the strawberries facing the outside of the cup.
4. Dollop about 2 tablespoons of crème on top of the cupcake.
5. Place the second strawberry over the top around the center.

OFFICE POTLUCK

- Curried Broccoli Crunch Salad
- Red Quinoa Roasted Pumpkin Salad with Asian Pears and Maple Glazed Pepitas
- Basmati Rice Salad with Ginger Miso Dressing
- Moon Dahl
- Chocolate Almond Filo Crispies
- Pumpkin Seed Dip with Veggie Crudité

*E*ach September we box up our white clothes and soak up the last bits of sun before waving goodbye to the summer breeze. But when we say farewell to one season's produce, we say hello to the harvest of another one. Soon enough, autumn will sweep in with a taste of its own.

So forget the cracker plate and fill your conference room with enticing seasonal aromas like pumpkin and maple. These all-inclusive dishes are simple enough to prep on a weeknight and substantial enough to serve buffet-style. So trade your blazer for an apron and get cracking on these all-but-typical potluck offerings.

CURRIED BROCCOLI CRUNCH SALAD

It's sweet, salty, crunchy and savory all in one dish. No matter who takes up the office space—from techies, to accountants, to creatives—this salad satisfies the cravings of every co-worker.

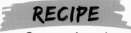
RECIPE

Serves 4 to 6

CURRIED SEITAN

1 pound	Original Seitan (page 41)	½ tsp.	toasted sesame oil
2 tbsp.	olive oil	3 tbsp.	curry powder

1. Cut seitan roasts into ½ x ½-inch pieces
2. Heat oil and toasted sesame oil in skillet and sauté seitan pieces with curry until lightly browned on all sides, about 4 minutes.
3. Remove from stove and let cool.

ASSEMBLY

½ pound	broccoli	½ cup	green onion, chopped
1 recipe	Curried Seitan	½ cup	cranberries
2 each	celery stalks	½ cup	vegan mayo
1 cup	cashews	1 tbsp.	maple syrup

1. Remove stems from broccoli and blanch quickly in ice water. Broccoli should be bright green.
2. Place seitan and broccoli in a large mixing bowl and mix well with other ingredients.

RED QUINOA ROASTED PUMPKIN SALAD WITH ASIAN PEARS AND MAPLE GLAZED PEPITAS

Some call quinoa the power protein, so don't be surprised when it quickly becomes CEO of this office potluck. The salad is suited up with Asian pear and pomegranate seeds, among other delights, so don't count on leftovers in the communal fridge.

RECIPE
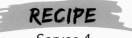
Serves 4

MAPLE GLAZED PEPITAS

½ cup	pumpkin seeds, raw	2 tsp.	maple syrup
2 tbsp.	water	¼ tsp.	chipotle juice (optional)
2 tsp.	soy sauce		

1. Over medium heat, roast pumpkin seeds in a dry skillet until lightly browned and popping.
2. While seeds are heating up, mix together water, soy sauce, maple syrup and chipotle juice (if desired).
3. When seeds are done browning pour in soy sauce mixture, reducing flame slightly. Let liquid start to evaporate. Stir, when mostly evaporated, to begin to dry seeds for about 1 minute.
4. Remove from heat and cool on baking sheet or flat plate.

SHALLOT CITRUS DRESSING

⅓ cup	olive oil	1 tbsp.	Dijon mustard
2 medium	shallots, peeled	½ tsp.	sea salt
3 tbsp.	orange juice	¼ tsp.	ground black pepper
1 tbsp.	lime juice		

1. In a 400°F oven, put olive oil and shallots in a small baking dish so oil covers shallots. Bake for 25 to 30 minutes until shallots are golden brown. Remove and let cool.
2. Put cooled shallots and olive oil in blender and add the rest of ingredients. Purée until well blended.

ASSEMBLY

1 whole	Kabocha squash (2 ½ to 3 pounds)	4 cups	mixed salad greens
		1 cup	Shallot Citrus Dressing
6 cups	red quinoa, cooked	1 cup	pomegranate seeds
1 cup	Italian parsley, chopped	½ cup	Maple Glazed Pepitas
1 whole	Asian pear, peeled		

1. Pre-heat oven to 400°F and place whole Kabocha in center and let bake for 45 minutes. Remove and let cool. Slice in half and remove seeds and stringy fibers, then gently peel off skin and slice in ½-inch cubes and set aside.
2. In a bowl, toss cooked quinoa with chopped Italian parsley.
3. Remove core from Asian pear and slice into ½-inch cubes.
4. Divide salad greens on serving plates and top with cubed Kabocha and Asian pear.
5. Drizzle dressing over and top with pomegranate seeds and Maple Glazed Pepitas.

BASMATI RICE SALAD
WITH GINGER MISO DRESSING

*C*ook it. Mix it. Eat it. This Asian-inspired salad is easy as 1-2-3. But with a maple, soy sauce and ginger dressing it's bound to make a lasting impression.

RECIPE
Serves 6

GINGER MISO VINAIGRETTE

½ cup	rice vinegar		2 tbsp.	olive oil
¼ cup	white miso		1 tbsp.	ginger, chopped
½ cup	green onion, chopped		2 tsp.	toasted sesame oil
3 tbsp.	maple syrup		⅛ tsp.	turmeric
2 tbsp.	soy sauce			

Put everything in a blender and blend.

ASSEMBLY

4 cups	Basmati rice, cooked and cooled		½ cup	frozen corn kernels, defrosted
1 whole	carrot, chopped in ¼-inch pieces		½ cup	green onions
1 cup	snow peas, sliced length-wise in ⅛-inch pieces		2 tbsp.	sesame seeds, toasted

1. Toss rice and vegetables together in large bowl to incorporate all ingredients.
2. Add Ginger Miso Vinaigrette and top with toasted sesame seeds.

MOON DAHL

This scoop-and-serve East Indian stew is thick with moong beans—a small, bright green-skinned legume that is a significant source of protein and fiber. Beans you say? Now don't jump ship so fast; these sturdy peas are known to be especially easy to digest.

RECIPE

Serves 4 to 6

1 cup	split moong dahl (available in import section or Indian markets)	1 tsp.	sea salt
		1 whole	tomato, chopped
		1 quarter	jalapeño, chopped
1 ½ cups	water	½ bunch	Swiss chard, chopped into ½-inch pieces
¼ cup	olive oil		
1 tbsp.	coconut oil	1 tsp.	lemon juice
1 ½ tsp.	cumin seeds	4 tbsp.	cilantro, chopped
1 ½ tsp.	coriander, ground	1 pinch	nutmeg, freshly ground
½ tsp.	turmeric		

1. Rinse beans well and sort through for stones.
2. Add water and bring to boil. Simmer for 30 minutes.
3. Heat olive and coconut oils and roast cumin seeds for 30 seconds. Add coriander, turmeric, salt, tomato and jalapeño and sauté for approximately three minutes.
4. Add Swiss chard and sauté another five minutes.
5. Add chard mixture to dahl.
6. Add lemon juice, chopped cilantro and freshly ground nutmeg.

CHOCOLATE ALMOND FILO CRISPIES

Use thin, flaky filo sheets to fold orange zest, chocolate and roasted almonds into this origami pastry. Their neat, palm-sized shape makes them a great pass-around snack.

RECIPE

Serves 8 to 12

1 cup	bittersweet chocolate	1 whole	orange, zested
½ cup	sugar	¼ cup	safflower oil
1 ½ cups	almonds, roasted and ground	15 sheets	filo dough

1. Preheat oven to 350°F.
2. Chop chocolate into ½-inch pieces and then place in blender with sugar.
3. Mix the chocolate mixture in a bowl with the almonds and orange zest.
4. Brush the bottom of a 9 x 13-inch pan with oil and place a sheet of filo brushed with oil on top.
5. Sprinkle the chocolate almond sugar mixture lightly over the top. Alternate filo sheet (with brushed oil), then chocolate, until all filo and mixture are used.
6. Using a sharp knife cut in squares or whatever shapes you would like to try!
7. Bake for 20 minutes or until nice and golden brown and crispy.

PUMPKIN SEED DIP WITH VEGGIE CRUDITÉ

Long days of paperwork require a lot of brainpower. Try this dip for a boost of zinc, magnesium and iron so you'll never fall asleep during a meeting again.

RECIPE
Serves 6

1 cup	water	2 whole	umeboshi plums, pits removed
1 cup	pumpkin seeds, raw or toasted	assortment of	carrot and celery sticks, cauliflower and broccoli florets, other veggies (your choice!)
1 tbsp.	tahini		
1 tsp.	sesame oil		

1. Place water, seeds, tahini, sesame oil and plums in blender and blend until smooth.
2. Place veggie crudité around dip and, well, dip away!

MAMA MIA PIZZERIA!

- Smoky Buffalo Pizza
- Double Cheeseburger Pizza
- Verdi's Roasted Veggie Pizza
- Very Voluptuous Veggie Pizza
- Sausage and Rapini Pizza

Pizzas have been with us through thick and thin (literally). From Saturday night deliveries to mid-week cravings—these pies are a big piece of our everyday lives. Not to mention all of the long-standing rivalries over who makes it best—New York thin, Chicago deep, California gourmet. And when something holds that much weight in our lives, it must be fêted.

Whether you grill yours out back or bake it in the oven, tonight's pizza should be a creation of your own, not a box from your neighborhood delivery guy. Pizza has always had a place in your heart, so put a little heart back into your pizza.

SMOKY BUFFALO PIZZA

We never quite understood why celery always pairs with "chicken" wings and ranch dressing, but throw them all together on a pizza pie with smoky buffalo, and you'll know why.

RECIPE

Makes 3- 10-inch pizzas

BUFFALO PIZZA SAUCE

2 cups	hot sauce	4 tbsp.	vegan margarine

1. Heat hot sauce in sauté pan on medium-high heat.
2. Add the butter and stir until it is melted.
3. Lower the heat from medium heat to low and allow the sauce to reduce by half, which will make it thicker.

BATTERED ORIGINAL SEITAN
Makes 1 patty

2 ounces	unsweetened, organic coconut milk	2 ounces	Original Seitan, rolled long ½-inch strips
¼ cup	unbleached organic flour	3 cups	vegetable oil

1. Place wax paper on the bottom of a sheet pan.
2. Put the milk in one bowl and the flour in another.
3. Saturate a patty in milk, then in the flour, covering it.
4. Dip the patty again into the milk and once again into the flour.
5. Fry seitan in a 350°F pot with oil for 3 to 3 ½ minutes.

ASSEMBLY

⅓ recipe	Pizza Dough (page 26)	½ cup	carrots, shredded
¼ cup	Buffalo Pizza Sauce	½ cup	celery, ¼-inch slices
2 patties	Battered Original Seitan	¼ cup	vegan ranch dressing
2 tbsp.	Buffalo Pizza Sauce	1 tbsp.	parsley, chopped
1 cup	romaine lettuce, shredded		

1. Brush pizza dough with Buffalo Pizza Sauce, leaving a ½-inch border.
2. Dice battered seitan into ½-inch pieces and spread them over the pizza.
3. Drizzle 2 tbsp. of Buffalo Sauce over the pizza.
4. Place in the middle of a 475°F oven for 4 to 5 minutes or until the edges are golden brown.
5. Place the lettuce evenly over the seitan. Then spread the carrots around the top of the lettuce.
6. Evenly distribute the celery and drizzle the ranch in a zigzag formation. Garnish with parsley.

DOUBLE CHEESEBURGER PIZZA

Makes 1- 10-inch pizza

⅓ recipe	Pizza Dough (page 26)	1 slice	vegan cheddar cheese
¼ tsp.	Roasted Garlic Oil (page 69)	2 slices	Roma tomato, chopped into ¼-inch pieces
2 ounces	marinara		
¾ cup	Original Setian (page 41), ground	4 slices	dill pickles, chopped into ¼-inch pieces
2 tbsp.	Caramelized Onions (page 85)	2 tbsp.	red onion, chopped
		2 tbsp.	sweet mustard

1. Brush pizza dough with Roasted Garlic Oil.
2. Spread marinara over crust evenly and top with ground seitan and onions.
3. Cut cheddar slice into 4 pieces on the diagonal and place on top of pizza, spreading out evenly over pizza.
4. Bake at 350°F for 10 minutes.
5. Sprinkle top with tomato, pickle and red onion.
6. Zigzag sweet mustard over the top.

VERDI'S ROASTED VEGGIE PIZZA

When the Verdi hits our eye, as a scrumptious pizza pie, that's amore.

RECIPE

Makes 1 pizza

⅓ recipe	Pizza Dough (page 26)	⅛ cup	fennel, grilled
1 tsp.	Roasted Garlic Oil (page 69)	⅛ cup	red onions, grilled
4 ounces	Tofu Ricotta (page 78)	6 cloves	Roasted Garlic (page 69)
⅛ cup	Roasted Cherry Tomatoes (page 13)	1 tbsp.	Basil Pesto (page 26)
⅛ cup	red peppers, grilled	1 ounce	Balsamic Glaze (page 72)

1. Brush top of dough with oil.
2. Spread Tofu Ricotta on top leaving ½-inch edges.
3. Spread tomatoes, peppers, fennel, onions and garlic evenly across the top.
4. Bake in oven for 10 minutes at 350°F.
5. Remove from oven. Garnish with pesto and glaze in a zigzag fashion.

VERY VOLUPTUOUS VEGGIE PIZZA

Your crispy crust and pesto might get lost under layers of grilled veggies in this "very voluptuous" pizza extravaganza. You may never find them, but your palate will taste it all.

RECIPE

ROASTED VEGGIES

½ cup	zucchini, pencil cut	½ cup	broccoli florets
½ cup	carrot, pencil cut	½ cup	yams, 1 x 1-inch pieces
½ cup	red bell peppers, deseeded, cut into ¼-inch pieces	½ tsp.	sea salt
		¼ tsp.	ground black pepper
½ cup	red onion, ¼-inch slices	¼ cup	olive oil
½ cup	cauliflower florets	¼ cup	water

1. Place the veggies in a mixing bowl with salt, pepper, olive oil and water.
2. Place the veggies on a baking sheet and place in the oven at 350°F. Roast for about 6 to 8 minutes.
3. Remove and let cool.

BALSAMIC VINAIGRETTE

1 tbsp.	yellow onion	½ tbsp.	sea salt
½ cup	balsamic vinegar	1 cup	olive oil
⅓ tbsp.	ground black pepper		

1. Peel and chop the yellow onions into ¼-inch pieces.
2. Place the vinegar and onions in blender, and purée until onions are liquefied.
3. Put mixture in a bowl and add black pepper and salt.
4. Mix with a hand-mixer on medium while gradually adding the olive oil to the mix. After all the oil is added, continue to mix for an additional 20 seconds.

ASSEMBLY

⅓ recipe	Pizza Dough (page 26)	1 tbsp.	Basil Pesto (page 26)
¼ tsp.	Roasted Garlic Oil (page 69)	1 cup	Steamed Kale (page 86)
		1 tsp.	Balsamic Vinaigrette
1 cup	Roasted Veggies	1 tbsp.	pumpkin seeds

1. Lightly brush the crust from edge to edge with garlic oil.

2. Chop veggies into ½-inch pieces.

3. Submerge kale in hot water for 10 to 15 seconds to reheat. Then lay to dry.

4. Drizzle pesto over crust and spread around, keeping ¼-inch border around the edge.

5. Sprinkle Roasted Veggies over the pizza.

6. Bake in 425°F oven for 5 minutes. Remove and add kale.

7. Drizzle Balsamic Vinaigrette in zigzag patterns over the pizza.

8. Garnish with pumpkin seeds.

SAUSAGE AND RAPINI PIZZA

Bring pizza to a new level of sophistication by topping it with seitan sausage and broccoli rabe. Even meat lovers will turn over a new plate for this healthy alternative.

RECIPE
Makes 3- 10-inch pizzas

ROASTED RED PEPPERS

2 whole   red peppers

Place peppers on the grill and grill each side for about 2 minutes, until charred. Remove from heat, let cool and peel the skin off. Julienne to equal about ½ cup.

BLANCHED RAPINI

2 cups   rapini, chopped

In a pot, bring ½ gallon of water to a boil and place rapini in water for 1 minute. Then shock in ice water. Remove from water and chop into 1-inch pieces.

If you're not making 3 pizzas, the dough freezes great! Just wrap tightly in plastic wrap and freeze. Take it out the night before to thaw in the refrigerator—we like this dough so much we sometimes double the recipe to have plenty to freeze—then easy peasy pizza!

ASSEMBLY
Makes 1 pizza

⅓ recipe	Pizza Dough (page 26)	1 tbsp.	Roasted Garlic (page 69)
¾ cup	tomato sauce		
1 cup	sausage seitan, ground	½ tsp.	dried oregano
⅓ recipe	Roasted Red Peppers	1 tbsp.	olive oil
1 cup	vegan mozzarella cheese, shredded	1 recipe	Blanched Rapini

1. Place 10-inch crust on baking sheet and brush with olive oil. Add tomato sauce all around the crust, leaving ½-inch border around the edge.
2. Sprinkle sausage seitan, roasted peppers rapini and cheese.
3. Bake in the oven for 10 minutes at 350°F.
4. Remove from oven and sprinkle with garlic and dried oregano.
5. Cut in 8 pieces.

TRICKS N' TREATS

- Candy Bar Bars
- Chewy Earth Bites
- Ghastly Gourd Parfaits
- Green Goo Goblin Stew
- Witches Warts with Ground Bones & Hearts Dipping Sauce
- Dragon's Blood Punch
- Grilled Cheese & Acorn Stew
- Goblin "Sweet" Bread Ginger Pudding
- Carmel Corn Tricky Treats
- Curried Pumpkin Apple Bisque
- Apple "Chai"der

Are you afraid of the dark? Then beware, because this spider web of recipes is creepy, crawly and gruesomely delicious. We realize the recipes sound a bit morbid—we're usually against blood, bones and skeletons when it comes to food—but since costumes and disguises are already on our minds, why not let food in on the fun?

Just hop on your broomstick, pull out your magic stirring wand and bewitch these ingredients into a deliciously dark concoction fit for warlocks and gremlins. It's a time for cooking and spooking—so eat, drink and be scary!

CANDY BAR BARS

*T*here will be no ghastly nightmares on Halloween's eve once this trail-mix treat fills your dreams with granola, chocolate chips and sweet currants.

RECIPE

Makes 12- 3 ounce pieces

CANDY CARAMEL SAUCE

3 cups	organic sugar	½ tsp.	sea salt
¼ cup	water	1 cup	vegan butter
2 ½ cups	soy milk	¼ cup	organic corn syrup
2 tsp.	vanilla		

1. Place the sugar, water, soy milk, vanilla, salt and butter in a medium-sized sauce pan on medium-high heat. Whisk until the butter is melted.
2. Whisk in the corn syrup and reduce heat to low. Cook on low heat until reduced by half.

COOKIE CRUST

1 ½ cups	vegan butter, melted	½ tsp.	sea salt
1 cup	organic sugar	2 tbsp.	ground jasmine rice
½ tsp.	vanilla	2 cups	unbleached organic flour

1. Place ingredients into a mixing bowl and mix well.
2. Evenly distribute the crust into an 8 x 8-inch baking pan and cook for 6 to 8 minutes at 350°F.
3. Remove and allow to cool.

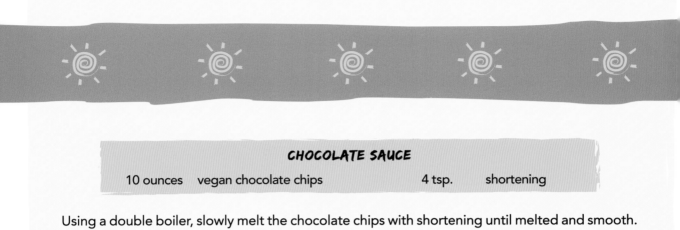

CHOCOLATE SAUCE

| 10 ounces | vegan chocolate chips | 4 tsp. | shortening |

Using a double boiler, slowly melt the chocolate chips with shortening until melted and smooth.

ASSEMBLY

| 1 recipe | Chocolate Sauce | 1 cup | peanuts, chopped |
| 1 recipe | Cookie Crust | 1 recipe | Candy Caramel Sauce |

1. Pour the melted chocolate over the crust and sprinkle with the chopped peanuts.
2. Drizzle the caramel sauce over the peanuts and allow to cool completely in the fridge.

CHEWY EARTH BITES

Don't be fooled, these bites may be disguised as earthy "dirt" globs, but underneath their costume is a sweet treat.

RECIPE
Makes 10 to 12 clods

1 ¼ cups	organic sugar	⅓ cup	peanut butter
½ cup	coconut milk	2 tsp.	vanilla
¼ cup	cocoa powder	1 ½ cups	quick rolled oats
⅓ cup	vegan butter	½ cup	salted peanuts

1. In a heavy skillet, mix sugar with coconut milk, cocoa powder, vegan butter, peanut butter and vanilla.
2. Put on medium heat and continue to whisk and stir until comes to boil and then let simmer 1 minute or two until nice and thickened.
3. Remove from heat and stir in rolled oats and salted peanuts.
4. Drop globs on lightly greased cookie sheet, let cool to harden.

GHASTLY GOURD PARFAITS

May this fall-flavored parfait rest in peace in your stomach after you "gourd-ge" on its creamy pumpkin filling and ginger spiced cookie crumble. Indeed you will be missed, parfait, but your spirit still lives on in our hearts.

RECIPE
Serves 5

PARFAIT

14 ounces	silken tofu, firm	1 tsp.	pumpkin pie spice
⅔ cup	maple syrup	½ cup	coconut oil, melted
1 can	organic pumpkin		

1. Add all ingredients into the blender.
2. Blend all ingredients (except coconut oil) together, and then on low speed, slowly add in the melted coconut oil.

COOKIE CRUMBLE

2 cups	unbleached organic flour	½ tsp.	ground cinnamon
1 tsp.	baking soda	½ cup	safflower oil
¼ tsp.	sea salt	¼ cup	molasses
1 cup	organic sugar	¼ cup	soy milk
2 ½ tbsp.	ground dry ginger	1 tsp.	vanilla

1. Sift the dry ingredients together in a bowl.
2. Combine all the wet ingredients together in a separate bowl.
3. Mix the dry with the wet using a whisk.
4. Roll the dough into little balls (about 1 inch in size). Slightly press down before cooking.
5. Bake at 350°F for 10 minutes.
6. Assemble by putting the parfait in the dish and topping with Cookie Crumble.

GREEN GOO GOBLIN STEW

When all the green veggies sink into this stew,
A dash of our magic will liven the brew.
The milk of the coconut, juice of the lime,
A pinch of the pepper and lemongrass fine,
Will bubble this cauldron with flavors so swell
That you'll stay entranced until lunch breaks the spell.

RECIPE

Serves 6

1 tbsp.	coriander seeds	1 cup	water
2 tsp.	cumin seeds	1 medium	zucchini, sliced in ¼-inch half moons
½ tsp.	whole black pepper		
1 tsp.	sea salt	¼ pound	green beans, ends trimmed and cut in 1-inch pieces
1 to 2 whole	jalapeños, chopped		
3 stalks	lemongrass, trimmed and finely chopped		
		14 ounces	silken tofu, firm and sliced in ¼-inch cubes
2 tbsp.	fresh ginger, chopped		
2 tbsp.	lime juice	1 ½ cups	cashews, whole
2 whole	limes, zest only	¼ cup	maple syrup
1 cup	spinach, chopped	1 tbsp.	soy sauce
2- 13 oz cans	coconut milk	½ tsp.	sea salt
		¼ tsp.	white pepper

GARNISH

1 cup	fresh basil, chiffonade	1 cup	fresh cilantro, chopped
6 wedges	lime		

Tip: Serve over black and white rice for added festivity

1. In a small skillet, heat coriander, cumin and whole black pepper to toast lightly.
2. With a mortar and pestle grind the freshly roasted spices.
3. Add the salt, jalapeños, lemongrass, ginger, lime juice and zest and continue to mash with mortar and pestle until it becomes a paste (if you don't have one, use a blender or coffee grinder for this step). Set aside.
4. In a blender, put in 6 tbsp. of paste, 1 cup chopped spinach and 1 can of coconut milk and purée.
5. In a stockpot, pour in the milk purée, water, zucchini, green beans, tofu and cashews. Simmer for 10 minutes.
6. Add maple syrup, soy sauce, salt and white pepper and simmer for another five minutes.
7. Serve over rice. Garnish with basil, lime wedges and cilantro.

WITCHES WARTS WITH GROUND BONES AND HEARTS DIPPING SAUCE

Keep remedies in your kitchen to ward off Halloween superstitions. If you fear the teeth of a vampire, grab this dish for its hint of garlic, and, feel free to have your own bite as you wait for the sun to fade.

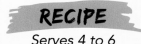

RECIPE

Serves 4 to 6

1 pound	baby Yukon Gold potatoes	1 clove	garlic
2 tbsp.	olive oil	¼ tsp.	smoked red paprika
¼ tsp.	coarse sea salt	¼ cup	mint
⅔ cup	almonds, roasted	¾ tsp.	coarse sea salt
2 medium	Roasted Red Peppers (page 291), peeled and seeded	2 tbsp.	olive oil

1. Preheat oven to 325°F.
2. Toss potatoes with olive oil and place on baking pan.
3. Sprinkle ¼ tsp. course sea salt on potatoes.
4. Bake for 1 ½ hours; do not turn.
5. Blend almonds (bones), roasted bell peppers (hearts), garlic, paprika, mint and ¾ tsp. course sea salt in blender. Then blend in olive oil.
6. Arrange potatoes on platter and serve alongside dip.

DRAGON'S BLOOD PUNCH

Serve this blood red beverage to all of your thirsty vampire friends.

RECIPE
Serves 15

1 ½ quarts	apple juice	1 ½ quarts	all-natural fruit punch or fruit juice blend
1 ½ quarts	cranberry juice		
2 liters	ginger ale	2 whole	oranges, zested

1. Combine all ingredients together and serve cold.
2. Perhaps add some Poisonous Berry or Orange Liquor for those grown-up witches and warlocks!

GRILLED CHEESE & ACORN SQUASH STEW

*H*alloween may be a holiday strictly for kids, but we're not big on rule-following at Native Foods. We're turning this holiday, along with our grilled cheese sandwich, into a party for young and old.

RECIPE
Serves 4

ACORN SQUASH BOWLS

4 medium	acorn squashes	1 tsp.	sea salt
2 tbsp.	olive oil		

1. Preheat the oven to 400°F.
2. Remove the top stem from the squash as well as the insides and the seeds, but save the body, including the top (like carving a pumpkin).
3. Rub the inside and outside of each acorn squash with the oil and sprinkle with salt. Place the squash on a baking sheet and roast until golden in the top but still keeping it's shape, about 20 to 25 minutes.
4. Set aside. They will be used for serving bowls.

STEW

½ cup	water (for sautéing)	1 tsp.	garlic powder
4 cloves	garlic, minced	½ tsp.	ground black pepper
½ cup	red onions, diced	¼ cup	vegan butter
½ cup	celery, diced	¼ cup	unbleached organic flour
½ cup	carrots, diced		
½ cup	sweet potatoes, diced	1 cup	red wine
½ cup	butternut squash, diced	3 cups	Vegetable Stock (page 17)
½ cup	purple potatoes, diced		
1 cup	sausage seitan, cubed	2 tbsp.	fresh thyme, chopped
1 tbsp.	sea salt		

1. Place the water in a large soup pan. Add the garlic, onion, celery and carrots and cook for 3 minutes on medium-high heat.
2. Add the sweet potato and butternut squash to the pan and cook for 3 more minutes. (You can always add more water if need be.)
3. Add the purple potatoes, seitan, salt, garlic powder, pepper and butter.
4. Once the butter is melted, add in the flour and "coat" the veggies with it.
5. Deglaze with the red wine and allow the liquid to reduce to cook off the alcohol.
6. Whisk the veggie stock and allow the stew to come to a soft boil. Then reduce the heat to medium and allow the stew to thicken and reduce in size.
7. Add the thyme at the end and serve in the Acorn Squash Bowls.

GHOSTS
Makes a small family of 'em

½ pound	Yukon Gold potatoes, washed and quartered	1 tsp.	sea salt
		2 tsp.	garlic powder
2 ½ quarts	water	20 to 22 whole	caper berries
1 tbsp.	vegan butter		or currants

1. Place the potatoes in a saucepan with 2 ½ quarts of water and bring to a boil.
2. Once the potatoes are fully cooked and fork tender, strain them carefully from the pan and place them in a bowl.
3. Mash the potatoes until they are smooth and lump free. Add the butter, salt and garlic powder.
4. Place the mashed potatoes in a gallon resealable bag and cut a dime-sized hole from the bottom.
5. Line a baking sheet with wax paper or parchment paper and create your ghostly friends! Use the caper or currants for the eyes but please don't stop there!

PUMPKIN GRILLED CHEESE
Makes 1

1 tbsp.	vegan butter	1 tsp.	olive oil
2 slices	multigrain bread	2 slices	vegan cheddar cheese
¼ cup	Caramelized Onions (page 85)	¼ cup	pumpkin butter

1. Heat the first butter in a sauté pan on medium-high heat. Place both pieces of bread in the pan and toast.
2. Place the onions either in the same pan (if there is room), or heat them up in a separate sauté pan on high heat with olive oil.
3. Flip the piece of bread over and toast on the other side. Place the 2 slices of cheese on one of the pieces of bread and spread the pumpkin butter over the other piece.
4. Arrange the onions over the cheese and close the sandwich up.
5. Allow the sandwich to heat in the pan until the cheese is melted.

GOBLIN "SWEET" BREAD GINGER PUDDING

Goblins are playing nice on Halloween with this sweet pudding of butternut squash, cinnamon and currants. But beware, once the clock strikes midnight, they're back to their usual mischief.

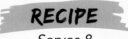

RECIPE
Serves 8

2 pounds	butternut squash	1 ½ tsp.	vanilla extract
2 cups	unsweetened soy milk	15 ounces	organic pumpkin purée
1 cup	brown sugar	1 loaf	bread (white or
1 ½ tsp.	cinnamon		cinnamon raisin)
½ tsp.	nutmeg	½ cup	currants or raisins
½ tsp.	ground allspice	¼ cup	crystallized ginger

1. Preheat oven to 375°F.
2. Cut squash in half. Remove the seeds. Brush the insides with a little oil and lay flat on a baking sheet, skin side up.
3. Roast in the preheated oven until soft all the way through, about 45 minutes to an hour. Remove from the oven and let cool.
4. When the squash is cool, remove the "flesh" and discard the skin, then purée in the blender. Set aside.
5. Reheat the oven to 350°F.
6. In a large bowl, combine the soy milk, brown sugar, spices and vanilla and mix well to combine.
7. Mix in the pumpkin and butternut squash purées.
8. Combine the bread, raisins and ginger in the 9 x 13-inch baking dish. Pour the pudding mixture over the bread to cover and let sit for 15 minutes.
9. Bake in the preheated oven until the pudding is set, about 20 to 25 minutes.

CARAMEL CORN TRICKY TREATS

When it comes to trick-or-treat, we always go for the treat. Munch away on this addicting caramel-coated popcorn while you settle in for a scary movie.

RECIPE

Makes one big bowl o' popcorn

½ cup	popcorn, unpopped	2 tbsp.	vegan butter
1 tsp.	sea salt	½ tsp.	maple syrup
¾ cup	brown sugar	¼ tsp.	vanilla
3 tbsp.	water		

1. Pop popcorn, and then sprinkle with sea salt.
2. Combine brown sugar, water, butter and maple syrup in saucepan and bring to a boil. Cover and boil on medium-low for 3 minutes.
3. Remove from heat, and then add vanilla. Let sauce cool just a tad, stirring constantly with spoon.
4. Pour over popped popcorn in a bowl and toss until well combined and glazed.

CURRIED PUMPKIN APPLE BISQUE

Don't be afraid to serve your guests something sophisticated even during this playful celebration. This bisque is a festive way to bring your guests back to earth after that sugar high and other-worldly fun.

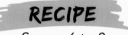

RECIPE

Serves 6 to 8

¼ cup	olive oil	2 to 3 lb.	pumpkin, or medium winter squash
2 cups	onions, chopped		
3 tbsp.	curry powder (optional)	6 cups	water
		2 ½ cup	coconut milk
2 cups	apples, chopped (or 1 cup applesauce)	2 ½ tbsp.	sea salt
		1 cup	pomegranate seeds

1. Bake pumpkin at 400°F for 45 minutes. Deseed, peel and chop.
2. Heat olive oil in a large saucepan and sauté onion until translucent and lightly browned.
3. Add curry powder and stir for 30 seconds. Add apples and cook for 1 minute.
4. Add pumpkin, water, coconut milk and salt.
5. Bring to boil then let simmer for 25 minutes. Cool slightly, then carefully purée in batches in blender.
6. Warm before serving and add pomegranate seeds.

APPLE "CHAI"DER

No need to bob for these apples—they're right here in your morning mug. So do yourself a solid and come down from the wild weekend with this cozy liquid.

RECIPE
Makes 2 gallons

CHAI TEA

10 cups	water	6 tbsp.	loose black tea
24 pods	cardamom	8 whole	cloves
¼ pound	ginger, cleaned and sliced	2 tsp.	ground nutmeg
6 sticks	cinnamon	1 whole	vanilla bean, cut in half
6 pieces	whole star anise	½ cup	Grade A maple syrup

1. Place everything in a large stockpot and bring to a simmer. DO NOT BOIL! Boiling black tea will result in a bitter taste.
2. Once at a simmer, allow the pot to continue to steep for 10 to 15 minutes more.
3. Then, using a strainer, carefully strain the liquid to remove all the aromatics.

ASSEMBLY

10 whole	Granny Smith apples, cut into 1-inch pieces	1 tbsp.	ground cinnamon
		1 tbsp.	allspice
1 gallons	water	1 recipe	Chai Tea, chilled
⅓ cup	maple syrup		

1. Chop apples into 1-inch pieces and place them into a stockpot.
2. Cover the apples with water and add the maple syrup, cinnamon and allspice.
3. Bring the pot to a boil and let go for 15 minutes.
4. Reduce the flame down to medium low and simmer. Allow the pot to simmer for 1 hour.
5. Strain the liquid into a large container making sure to keep all the apple chunks out of the container. (Use the apples for a delicious applesauce.)
6. Add the Chai Tea to the apple cider and cool completely.

THANKS AND GIVING

- Candied Cranberries
- Fresh and Lively Brussels Sprout Hazelnut Salad
- Grandma's Green Bean Casserole
- Potato Fennel Gratin
- Chestnut and Butternut Squash Stuffing
- Fig n' Raspberry Cranberry Sauce
- Pumpkin Cheesecake
- Wild Rice Pilaf with Butternut Squash and Cranberries
- Pear and Cranberry Upside Down Cake
- Creamy Peppercorn Sauce

We know what you're thinking. Thanksgiving without a turkey is no Thanksgiving at all. But Native Foods knows plenty of ways to fill tummies without frying our feathered friends, and we're sharing them, from our table to yours.

These recipes are revitalized takes on an old and familiar menu. Like our predecessors, we give thanks for the earth's bounty after the harvest and use as many seasonal crops as we can. From golden squash to deep red cranberries, our cornucopia of ingredients is spilling over with autumn colors and flavors, and we've nowhere to put them but on your plates.

CANDIED CRANBERRIES

We let this favorite tradition have a little fun all on its own—as a sugarcoated treat, not just as a garnish.

RECIPE

Makes 1 ½ cups

1 cup	water	2 cups	frozen cranberries
1 cup	organic sugar	½ cup	organic sugar for dusting

1. In a saucepan, add the water and 1 cup of sugar. Cook on medium heat for 8 minutes.
2. Add frozen cranberries and cook for 2 minutes.
3. Strain the cranberries from the syrup.
4. Toss the wet cranberries in a bowl with the ½ cup of sugar.
5. Once the cranberries are coated, place them on wax paper lining a half sheet pan.
6. Allow them to cool for at least 2 hours.

FRESH AND LIVELY BRUSSELS SPROUT HAZELNUT SALAD

*T*he orange zest and apple cider vinegar give a creative edge to Brussels sprouts, and the result might be just enough to get the kids hooked on this veggie for good.

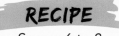

RECIPE

Serves 6 to 8

1 ½ lbs.	Brussels sprouts	2 tbsp.	apple cider vinegar
6 cups	water	2 tbsp.	orange juice
1 tbsp.	coarse sea salt	2 tbsp.	orange zest
¼ cup	sunflower or olive oil	3 tbsp.	maple syrup
2 tbsp.	shallots, peeled and chopped	¼ tsp.	sea salt
2 tbsp.	Dijon mustard	1 cup	hazelnuts, toasted, slightly chopped
2 tbsp.	whole grain Dijon		

1. Wash and trim ends from the Brussels sprouts.
2. Bring 8 cups of water with 1 tbsp. of coarse salt to a boil.
3. Add Brussels sprouts and cook for 4 minutes.
4. Drain and let dry.
5. Thinly slice Brussels sprouts by hand or by food processor after cooled.
6. In a blender, purée ¼ cup oil with the shallot. Then pour into bowl and whisk in the rest of the ingredients (except hazelnuts).
7. Toss dressing with sliced Brussels sprouts and top with toasted hazelnuts.

GRANDMA'S GREEN BEAN CASSEROLE

*T*he serotonin levels in these creamy, breaded green beans will have you in a state of content for much of the evening. Someone may even have to casser-"roll" you off the couch for dessert.

RECIPE

Serves 6 to 8

1 pound	green beans, trimmed	2 tsp.	olive oil
½ cup	olive oil	½ lbs	button mushrooms, sliced
2 cups	shallots, sliced		
½ cup	organic all-purpose flour	½ tsp.	sea salt
2 cloves	garlic, minced	1 cup	rice or almond milk
2 cups	panko breadcrumbs	¾ cup	vegan mayo
		¼ tsp.	ground black pepper

1. Blanch green beans in salted boiling water for 5 to 6 minutes, drain and put in ice bath to shock and hold color, then drain.
2. Heat olive oil in a skillet until hot.
3. Toss shallot slices in flour. Remove excess flour and fry until golden. When done, remove with slotted spoon.
4. In the same pan, heat garlic until just golden brown. Remove from heat and add breadcrumbs. Mix well and set aside.
5. In another skillet, heat 2 tsp. of olive oil until hot. Add sliced mushrooms and salt. Cook until slightly dry and golden brown.
6. Whisk non-dairy milk with mayo and black pepper. Pour into pan with mushrooms and stir.
7. Remove from heat, add green beans and bread crumbs.
8. Toss and serve!

POTATO FENNEL GRATIN

This year we're grateful for gratin. We're grateful for the cashew cream, caramelized fennel and sweet apples that make the gratin. Oh, and we are also thankful for our friends and family (as long as they do not eat all the gratin).

RECIPE
Serves 8

POTATOES AND FENNEL

2 pounds	Yukon gold potatoes	½ cup	yellow onion, sliced thinly
2 tbsp.	olive oil		
2 bulbs	fresh fennel, sliced thinly lengthwise	¼ tsp.	sea salt
		¼ tsp.	white pepper

1. Preheat oven to 350°F.
2. Fill a pot with enough water to cover the potatoes. Boil potatoes for 30 minutes. Drain, then let cool and peel. Set aside.
3. Heat olive oil in skillet. Add sliced fennel, onion, ¼ tsp. salt and white pepper. Sauté slowly until golden brown and caramelized, then remove from heat.

CREAMY CASHEWS

2 cups	cashews, soaked in 2 cups hot water for 20 minutes	1 clove	garlic
		1 tsp.	sea salt
2 cups	water	1 whole	lemon, zested

1. Drain the water from soaking cashews.
2. Blend cashews, water, garlic, salt and lemon zest in a blender until creamy.

ASSEMBLY

1 recipe	Potatoes and Fennel	2 tbsp.	olive oil
1 recipe	Creamy Cashews	2 cloves	garlic, minced
¾ cup	apples, cored and sliced thinly	2 cups	breadcrumbs
		¼ tsp.	sea salt

1. Thinly slice potatoes into rounds, place in a bowl and toss with Creamy Cashews.
2. Layer potatoes so they're slightly overlapping in a 9 x 13-inch pan (or some size close to that), then top with fennel-onion mixture and spread evenly.
3. Place apple slices on top of fennel-onion mixture.
4. Layer the rest of the potatoes on top and any remaining cream left in bowl or blender. Use a spatula so you get it all!
5. In a skillet, heat olive oil and add minced garlic. Remove from heat when lightly browned and add breadcrumbs and salt. Mix well.
6. Top entire dish with breadcrumbs and bake for 40 to 50 minutes.

CHESTNUT AND BUTTERNUT SQUASH STUFFING

Despite the big to-do about turkey, everyone knows that a good stuffing is the real star of a traditional Thanksgiving meal. And this show-stealing side dish is the definition of good. Don't believe us? Just try it.

RECIPE
Serves 6 to 8

4 cups	roasted butternut squash	1 tbsp.	garlic, small chopped
2 tbsp.	olive oil	1 tbsp.	thyme, chopped
1 tsp.	sea salt	1 cup	dried cranberries
½ tsp.	ground black pepper	1 tsp.	paprika
1 cup	carrots, medium diced	2 tbsp.	vegan butter
1 cup	onions, medium diced	1 cup	Native Bacon
2 cups	button mushrooms, small chopped		(page 23), chopped
		8 cups	bread, diced into small cubes
1 cup	chestnuts, small chopped		

1. In a bowl, mix the squash with olive oil, salt and pepper. Place on a sheet pan and bake in the oven for 10 minutes at 350°F. Remove and let cool.

2. In a 12-inch sauté pan, add oil mixture, carrots, onions, mushrooms, chestnuts, garlic, thyme, cranberries, paprika, butter and Native Bacon. Cook for about 10 minutes on low heat. Then remove from heat and let cool.

3. Place all ingredients in a mixing bowl, then add the breadcrumbs and mix well. Place mixture in a casserole dish and bake in oven for about 10 minutes at 350°F. Remove and let cool.

FIG N' RASPBERRY CRANBERRY SAUCE

*T*ip: This sweet side dish tastes better the day after. Make it a day early and have one less thing to worry about the morning-of.

RECIPE

Makes 3 ½ cups

1 ⅔ cup	ruby Port	1 cup	fresh organic raspberries
¼ cup	balsamic vinegar	1 sprig	fresh rosemary
¼ cup	organic brown sugar, packed	12 oz	fresh or frozen cranberries, thawed
8 whole	fresh figs, cut in half and stems removed	¾ cup	organic cane sugar
		¼ tsp.	ground black pepper

1. Combine the first 6 ingredients in a medium saucepan. Bring to boil, stirring until brown sugar dissolves.
2. Reduce heat to low and simmer for 10 minutes. Discard rosemary.
3. Mix in cranberries, ¾ cup sugar and pepper. Cook over medium heat until liquid is slightly reduced and berries burst, stirring occasionally, about 6 minutes.
4. Transfer sauce to bowl; chill until cold.

PUMPKIN CHEESECAKE

Pumpkin pie turned cheesecake? What could be better? And after a marathon day of eating under your belt, what's one more sliver of heaven added to the mix?

RECIPE

Makes 1 cheesecake

MAPLE PECAN CARAMEL SAUCE

1 cup	organic brown sugar	1 tbsp.	vegan butter
¼ cup	rice milk	½ tbsp.	vanilla extract
2 tbsp.	maple syrup	1 ¼ tsp.	applewood smoked salt
¼ cup	coconut milk	½ cup	pecan pieces, toasted

1. In saucepan, place brown sugar, rice milk and maple syrup. Whisk together well over medium heat and bring to a boil.
2. Turn heat from medium to low and let simmer for 12 minutes while whisking.
3. Remove from heat and add the coconut milk, butter, vanilla and smoked salt.
4. Return to heat and stir while simmering for another 2 minutes.
5. Remove from heat and stir in toasted pecans. Let cool before serving.

ASSEMBLY

5 tbsp.	vegan butter	4 tbsp.	tapioca starch
2 cups	vegan granola, ground	2 tsp.	vanilla extract
1 cup	vegan sour cream	1 ½ tsp.	pumpkin pie spice
1 cup	vegan cream cheese	⅛ tsp.	sea salt
¾ cup	pumpkin purée	1 recipe	Maple Caramel Sauce
⅓ cup	organic sugar		

1. Slowly melt vegan butter in a saucepan.
2. Place the ground granola in a mixing bowl and pour melted butter on top. Mix well.
3. Press granola mixture into a pie pan and evenly distribute around the pie pan.
4. Combine all the rest of the ingredients (except Maple Pecan Caramel Sauce) in a mixing bowl and blend with a hand mixer until smooth and creamy.
5. Pour into prepared piecrust.
6. Bake for 25 minutes at 325°F.
7. Let cool for 2 hours, then place in fridge and cool another 2 hours.
8. Serve with Maple Pecan Caramel Sauce

WILD RICE PILAF WITH BUTTERNUT SQUASH AND CRANBERRIES

Just like our turkeys, we prefer our rice wild, and paired with the season's most colorful offerings. This warm side dish is so good it might distract the mouths of even the chattiest aunts and uncles for the evening.

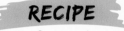

RECIPE
Serves 6

2 tbsp.	water	1 cup	wild rice
1 cup	onion, diced in small pieces	1 cup	brown rice
½ cup	carrots, diced in small pieces	2 whole	Bartlett Pears, peeled and diced
1 tbsp.	fresh ginger, minced	1 stick	cinnamon
2 cloves	garlic, chopped	3 ¾ cups	Vegetable Stock (page 17)
1 tsp.	curry powder	1 cup	dried cranberries
1 tsp.	cumin	to taste	sea salt
3 cups	butternut squash, cut in ½-inch cubes		

1. Heat the water, onion and carrots in a pot. Cook for 4 minutes or until tender.
2. Add the ginger, garlic, curry powder and cumin. Cook for 2 more minutes, stirring.
3. Add butternut squash, both types of rice, diced pears, cinnamon stick and stock.
4. Bring the pot to a boil, cover and reduce the heat to a simmer. Cook until the rice is tender, about 45 minutes.
5. Take the pot off the heat and stir in the dried cranberries.
6. Add salt and adjust seasonings if needed
7. Serve warm and enjoy!

PEAR CRANBERRY UPSIDE DOWN CAKE

Your kitchen is probably upside down after feeding the family, which might explain why your cake is too. We're head-over-heels for this upside down cake, which incorporates fresh orange zest and baked pecans.

RECIPE
Serves 8

½ cup	brown sugar	¼ tsp.	sea salt
¼ cup	vegan margarine	⅓ cup	safflower or sunflower oil
½ cup	pecan halves	¾ cup	organic sugar
4 whole	Bartlett Pears	7 ounces	silken tofu, firm
2 tbsp.	vegan margarine	½ cup	orange juice
2 cups	fresh cranberries	1 whole	orange, zested
1 ½ cups	unbleached flour	1 tsp.	vanilla extract
2 ½ tsp.	baking powder		

1. Preheat oven to 350°F.
2. Use a fork or your fingers to mash brown sugar and a ¼ cup of margarine into the bottom of an 8 x 8-inch or 9-inch round baking pan.
3. Place pecan halves randomly on bottom.
4. Peel pears, slice in quarters and remove core, then slice into eighths.
5. Heat 2 tbsp. of non-dairy margarine in skillet and sauté skin side up for 1 to 2 minutes on each side.
6. Arrange sautéed pears on bottom of baking dish.
7. Pour cranberries evenly over top of pears and make sure to fill the gaps between pear slices with cranberries.
8. In a bowl, mix together the flour, baking powder and salt.
9. Purée the rest of the ingredients in a blender.
10. Mix liquid into dry ingredients and spoon batter evenly over parts.
11. Bake for 35 to 40 minutes.
12. Let cool, then invert on serving plate and gently tap to loosen cake.

CREAMY PEPPERCORN SAUCE

This savory peppercorn sauce is just the thing for slathering seitan, stuffing and whatever else your heart desires. Fill up your best gravy boat and let it sail around the table a few times.

RECIPE

Serves 4

½ cup	cashews, raw	1 cup	yellow onion, diced
1 ½ cups	water	1 tsp.	garlic, minced
3 tbsp.	nutritional yeast	3 tbsp.	black peppercorns
2 tbsp.	olive oil	to taste	sea salt

1. Grind the cashews to a powder in the blender, and then add the water, yeast and olive oil. Blend until smooth.
2. Heat a pan over low-medium heat and sauté the onions for 3 minutes until they're soft. Add a little water or more oil if they're too dry.
3. Add the garlic and the peppercorns. Cook for about 1 more minute. Add to cashew mixture in blender and blend again until smooth and creamy.
4. Pour into saucepan, add salt to taste, and heat over low heat for about 5 to 8 minutes or until it gets thick and creamy.
5. Serve hot and enjoy!

Chapter Twelve: December

THE COOKIE EXCHANGE

- Chocolate Chip Cookie Dough Macaroons
- German Chocolate Cake
- Gluten-Free Rocky Road Brownies
- Dancing Gingerbread Cookies
- Gingerbread Cheesecake

Picture an entire table—no two tables—covered from corner to corner with cookie creations. Gingerbreads, macaroons, brownies—you name it. They're all in attendance and they're all yours to eat. That's the magic of a Cookie Exchange.

In the throes of a white winter, treats are on everyone's mind, and crowded exchanges are sure to come up. Go to socialize and sample whatever morsels you can get your hands on. The catch? You've got to bring a tray of your own.

No need to stress (save that for gift shopping)—these original vegan recipes are sure to stand out among the masses. Technically they're not all cookies, but who says you can't mix it up? We're not biased when it comes to our sweet tooth.

CHOCOLATE CHIP COOKIE DOUGH MACAROONS

With just five items on the ingredient list, this no-bake recipe gets whipped up and scooped out faster than a snowball. Let the rounded spoonfuls chill for a few hours before toting them along to your next event.

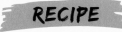

RECIPE

Makes 8-10, 1-tbsp. balls

⅔ cup	cashews, raw	1 tsp.	vanilla extract
⅓ cup	oats	¼ cup	mini vegan chocolate chips
2 ½ tbsp.	agave nectar		

1. Blend cashews and oats (in a blender or food processor) until a flour is created.
2. Add agave and vanilla to the flour and blend some more until a dough ball has formed.
3. Remove dough ball, place on clean surface and fold in chocolate chips with your hands.
4. Roll into bite-size balls and chill for a couple of hours. These freeze well too!

GERMAN CHOCOLATE CAKE

Despite its name, this two-layered cake is actually an American tradition, named after American chocolate maker Sam German. Foreign or not, it tastes like home to us. Pre-slice it before you go, to make for simpler sampling.

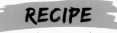

RECIPE

Makes 1 cake

CAKE

3 ½ cups	unbleached organic flour	1 ½ cups	cocoa powder
4 tsp.	baking powder	1 cup	safflower oil
2 tsp.	baking soda	3 cups	maple syrup
2 tsp.	sea salt	1 tsp.	apple cider vinegar
2 cups	soy milk	1 tsp.	vanilla extract

1. Preheat the oven to 350°F. Make sure to have 2 round 8-inch non-stick pans ready.
2. In a bowl, sift together the flour, baking powder, baking soda and salt.
3. Heat the soy milk on low in a small pan. When bubbling, remove from heat and add the cocoa powder, then whisk together.
4. In another bowl, combine the oil, maple syrup, vinegar and vanilla. Pour in the cocoa mixture and whisk until smooth.
5. Pour evenly into the two round pans and bake for 25 to 30 minutes. Let cool completely.

COCONUT FROSTING

½ cup	soy milk	1 tsp.	vanilla extract
¼ cup	cornstarch	3 cups	unsweetened shredded coconut
2 cups	organic brown sugar		
1 ½ cups	coconut milk	1 cup	pecans, chopped

1. For the frosting, whisk the soymilk and cornstarch together.
2. In a saucepan, on medium heat, dissolve the brown sugar in the coconut milk, continually whisking until the mixture comes to a boil.
3. Then reduce the heat to low and simmer for 5 minutes, or until slightly thickened.
4. Stir in the soy milk mixture and whisk continuously until the mixture is very thick and smooth.
5. Remove from the heat and fold in the vanilla, coconut and pecans. Let cool completely before assembling the cake.

ASSEMBLY

1. Remove cake from pans. Lay one of the cakes on a cake stand.
2. Spread ½ recipe of Coconut Frosting on top of the cake-stand cake. (Do not cover the sides.)
3. Place the second cake on top of the first, with rounded side facing up.
4. Spread the rest of the frosting on top of the second cake (again, not on the sides).
5. Slice and enjoy.

GLUTEN-FREE ROCKY ROAD BROWNIES

The road to happiness is paved with pecans, white chocolate and vegan marshmallows. So as you might imagine, it's pretty rocky. Bake a double batch of these sharable squares—they won't stay in the pan long.

RECIPE

Makes 1 pan

1 cup	gluten-free flour	½ cup	non-dairy milk
½ tsp.	baking soda	1 tsp.	vanilla extract
½ tsp.	sea salt	¼ cup	vegan chocolate chips
½ cup	cocoa powder	¼ cup	vegan white chocolate chips
1 cup	organic sugar		
14 ounces	silken tofu	½ cup	chopped pecans
½ cup	safflower oil	1 ½ cups	mini vegan marshmallows

1. Preheat oven to 350°F and grease an 8 x 8-inch baking pan with a non-stick spray or oil.
2. In a large bowl, combine the gluten-free flour, baking soda, salt, cocoa powder and sugar.
3. In a blender or food processor, combine tofu, safflower oil, milk and vanilla and blend until smooth.
4. Add the wet mixture into the dry ingredients and mix until just combined. Add in the chocolate chips, pecans and marshmallows.
5. Pour batter into pan. The marshmallows tend to bubble up so place a large cookie sheet or foil under the brownie pan. Bake for 45 to 60 minutes or until a toothpick or knife inserted into the middle comes out clean.

DANCING GINGERBREAD COOKIES

If gingerbread men live in gingerbread houses, than these elegant circle cookies must live in a gingerbread palace. Touched with pumpkin spice and topped with candied ginger, these bites bring a big batch of warmth into your chilly winter wonderland.

RECIPE

Makes 10 to 12 cookies

2 ½ cups	unbleached organic flour	½ tsp.	sea salt
1 tbsp.	baking soda	¾ cup	maple syrup
1 tbsp.	baking powder	½ cup	safflower oil
2 tsp.	ginger powder	¼ cup	molasses
1 tsp.	pumpkin pie spice	1 cup	candied ginger, chopped

1. Preheat oven to 375°F.
2. Mix flour, baking soda, baking powder, ginger, pumpkin pie spice and salt together in a bowl.
3. Stir in the rest of the ingredients, except the candied ginger, using a whisk to form a sticky dough.
4. Lightly oil two cookie sheets.
5. Using a melon baller scoop, place scoops of dough on sheet pans and separate by 1 inch.
6. Place a few pieces of candied ginger on top of each scoop of dough and lightly press down.
7. Bake for 10 minutes, let cool and enjoy with a cup of non-dairy milk.

GINGERBREAD CHEESECAKE

If you're already whipping up the gingerbread cookies, you may as well go the extra step and make this cheesecake too. Just add a pie pan, some creamy filling, and presto!

RECIPE
Makes 1 cheesecake

⅓ cup	vegan butter	⅛ cup	molasses
3 ⅓ cups + ½ cup	Dancing Gingerbread Cookie crumbs (see previous recipe)	2 tsp.	pumpkin pie spice
		½ tsp.	ground ginger
		1 tbsp.	fresh ginger, finely chopped
2 cups	vegan cream cheese		
1 cup	vegan sour cream	¼ tsp.	sea salt
¼ cup	maple syrup	1 tbsp.	orange zest

1. Slowly melt the vegan butter in a saucepan. Place the 3 ⅓ cups cookie crumbs in a mixing bowl, pour the melted butter over the cookie crumbs and mix well.
2. Press cookie crumb mixture into pie pan and evenly distribute into a round pie pan.
3. In a large bowl combine all ingredients (except remaining cookie crumbs) and mix with a hand blender until smooth and creamy. Alternatively, you can place in a blender and blend until smooth and creamy.
4. Pour into prepared crust.
5. Sprinkle the remaining cookie crumbs on top and bake at 275°F for 35-40 minutes.

SEASON'S EATINGS

- Red Chard and Ricotta Burek
- Polenta Pesto Bites
- Savory Stuffed Mushrooms
- Native Escalivada
- Almond Holiday Nog
- Cheeseball
- Wild Mushroom Fricassee on Garlic Toasted Crostini

There's "snow" place like home for the holidays, and nothing better than bringing together a flurry of your nearest and dearest around some jolly good food. 'Tis the season for giving and, frankly, for eating, so stop crossing off your gift-giving checklist and focus on your grocery list. Don't forget to check both of them twice!

You'll have guests dashing through the snow for their first bite of these holiday classics. And, baby it's cold outside, so make their trek worth it. Entertain with finger foods and share the season's bounty.

RED CHARD AND RICOTTA BUREK

Give the perfect gift with this stuffed pastry filled with tofu ricotta and vitamin-dense greens. This recipe serves a crowd and makes every spirit bright.

RECIPE
Serves 12 to 15

1 pound	silken tofu	¼ tsp.	ground black pepper
¼ cup	basil, chiffonade	1 bunch	red chard
¼ cup	Italian parsley, chopped	3 tbsp.	olive oil
¼ cup	green onions, chopped	1 cup	yellow onion, thinly sliced
2 cloves	garlic, minced	¼ tsp.	sea salt
2 tsp.	tahini	¼ cup	olive oil
1 tsp.	sea salt	½ pound	filo dough, defrosted

1. Preheat oven to 375°F.
2. Crumble tofu in a bowl to resemble cottage cheese. Add basil, parsley, green onions, garlic, tahini, salt and pepper. Mix until it resembles ricotta consistency and set aside.
3. Separate stems from leaves of chard. Cut stems into ½-inch pieces and leaves into ½-inch strips.
4. Heat 2 tbsp. of olive oil in a skillet and sauté onions with ¼ tsp. salt until transparent and lightly browned, then add stems and stir for about 1 to 2 minutes.
5. Place chard greens on top and turn flame to medium. When greens wilt, stir into stem and onion mix and let sauté for about another 3 minutes.
6. Remove from heat.
7. Have a pastry brush in a cup with the ¼ cup olive oil. Unroll filo and cover with a damp cloth.
8. Oil lightly the bottom of a 9 x 13-inch pan. Place two pieces of filo on top and brush with oil. Repeat 4 more times until you have used about 10 filo sheets.

9. Spread ricotta mix over bottom and top with sautéed chard.
10. Repeat the filo layering on top.
11. Cut squares with a sharp knife.
12. Bake 40 to 50 minutes until golden brown.
13. Serve warm or at room temperature.

POLENTA PESTO BITES

You'll have anything but a silent night when these bites get passed around and the room starts buzzing. Variations include adding some chopped rosemary or some fresh lemon zest to the polenta at the end

RECIPE
Makes 10 to 14 bites

5 cups	water		½ cup	pine nuts, toasted
2 tsp.	sea salt		2 cloves	garlic, chopped
1 cup	polenta		1 tsp.	sea salt
⅓ cup	olive oil		½ tsp.	lemon juice
1 cup	basil leaves		12 whole	teardrop tomatoes, halved
½ cup	olive oil			

1. In a large saucepan bring water to boil. Add salt and gradually add the corn meal, stirring constantly with a whisk.
2. Turn to medium low. Whisk in olive oil and let simmer while stirring until mixture thickens, about 10 to 12 minutes.
3. Pour the mixture into a 9 x 13-inch pan and let sit until firm. Set aside.
4. Put pine nuts, garlic, salt and lemon juice in a blender and blend until puréed.
5. Cut polenta into small squares. (Or cut into shapes if you have a small cookie cutter set!)
6. Top with a dollop of pesto and half slice of tear drop tomatoes.

SAVORY STUFFED MUSHROOMS

'Tis the season to be freezin', so warm up by the open fire with these savory button mushrooms.

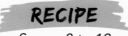

RECIPE

Serves 8 to 12

2 dozen medium	button mushrooms	½ cup	rice milk
4 whole	shallots, minced	½ tsp.	sea salt
4 tbsp.	olive oil	¼ tsp.	black pepper
¼ cup	ground hazelnuts	2 tbsp.	fresh rosemary, finely chopped

1. Preheat oven to 375°F.
2. Carefully remove the stems from the mushroom caps and finely chop the mushroom stems.
3. Sauté shallots and chopped mushroom stems in olive oil in skillet until translucent and lightly browned.
4. Add hazelnuts and sauté another minute.
5. Stir in rice milk, salt and pepper.
6. Remove from flame and add chopped rosemary.
7. Place mushroom caps on oiled 9 x 13-inch baking dish.
8. Fill them with a tsp. and bake for 15 minutes.

Tastes great with dill cream. Mix ½ cup vegan mayo
with fresh chopped dill to taste.

NATIVE ESCALIVADA

Good tidings we bring with this red and green colored veggie dish. Escalivada is often used as a sort of relish, so lay it over crusty breads, seitan or something new and different.

RECIPE

Makes 12 to 16 bites

½ cup	cashews, soaked		1 whole	Roasted Red Pepper (page 291)
¼ cup	currents, soaked		1 tbsp.	balsamic vinegar
½ pound	small eggplant, peeled, sliced ½-inch thick		¼ cup	olive oil
2 tbsp.	olive oil		2 tbsp.	parsley, chopped
1 tsp.	sea salt		1 tbsp.	fresh thyme, chopped
½ cup	Caramelized Onions (page 85)		2 tbsp.	capers, drained
			to garnish	parsley, chopped

1. Let the cashews and currants soak, separately, in water for at least 4 hours.
2. Peel and slice the eggplant, lengthwise, about ¼-inch thick. Lay all slices out and brush both sides with oil.
3. Season with salt and pepper on both sides. Grill each side for 1½ minutes. Make sure that the eggplant isn't burnt, but also not raw. Set aside to cool.
4. Mix the caramelized onions, roasted peppers, vinegar, oil, parsley, thyme and capers together in a bowl. Set aside.
5. Drain cashews and currants. In a blender, add the drained cashews, capers, salt and oil. Should turn out to be a smooth spreadable mix.
6. Cut the eggplant into rounds or squares (your preference), and spread 1 tsp. of the cashew cream on the top of each eggplant piece. Then add a dollop of the onion pepper mix. Garnish with chopped parsley.

ALMOND HOLIDAY NOG

No eggs in this nog! Even so, guests could get carried away with this sweet seasonal treat. Serve it cool and let the merriment begin!

RECIPE
Serves 4

6 cups	unsweetened vanilla almond milk	2 tbsp.	vanilla extract
		1 tsp.	nutmeg
⅓ cup	agave nectar	1 tsp.	cinnamon

Whisk together, or put in a blender and buzzzzzzz…

CHEESEBALL

Round as a snowball, this savory kitchen cheeseball is too delicious to throw at just anyone.

RECIPE
Makes 1 cheeseball

1 cup	almonds, slivered and blanched	1 tsp.	horseradish
		1 tsp.	red wine vinegar
¼ cup	pine nuts, unsalted and toasted	1 tsp.	lemon juice
		1 tsp.	safflower oil
¼ tsp.	sea salt	½ tsp.	onion powder
½ tsp.	organic sugar	1 tsp.	fresh chives, chopped
5 ounces	silken tofu, firm and drained	¾ cup	walnuts, finely chopped and toasted (to coat outside)
1 tbsp.	white miso paste		

1. Place almonds and pine nuts in a food processor with the salt and sugar and blend until ground for about 2 minutes or until clumps start to form.
2. Now add the tofu, miso paste and horseradish to the nut mixture that's already in the food processor, along with the red wine vinegar, lemon juice, safflower oil and onion powder. Blend about 2 minutes.
3. Gently fold the chives in with a fork or spoon.
4. Spray a bowl and a square of plastic wrap with no-stick spray. Pile mixture into the bowl and cover with plastic wrap. Place in fridge to chill for couple of hours or overnight. It will get very firm and can now be shaped into a ball and rolled in chopped walnuts to coat. Lightly oil your hands so it will not stick when rolling…. Then serve with crackers and wine.

WILD MUSHROOM FRICASSEE ON GARLIC TOASTED CROSTINI

Your halls may be decked with holly, but this fricassee is decked out with as many mushroom varieties as we could get our hands on.

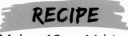

RECIPE

Makes 12 to 16 bites

1 mini	baguette, 6-inches long	½ pound	Chanterelles or lobster mushrooms
¼ cup	Garlic Oil (page 69)		
1 pound	shitakes, cleaned and stems removed	2 cloves	garlic, minced
		2 whole	shallots, minced
1 pound	Portobello mushrooms, cleaned, diced ¼- inch	2 tsp.	sea salt
		½ tsp.	black pepper, cracked
1 pound	maitake mushrooms	¼ cup	vegan sour cream
½ pound	king or oyster mushrooms		

1. Preheat oven 350°F.
2. Slice baguette into ¼-inch slices. Brush with garlic oil.
3. Toast for 9 to 11 minutes or until golden brown.
4. Clean all mushrooms and dice into ½-inch pieces.
5. Heat sauté pan up on medium-high heat. Add 2 tbsp. garlic oil.
6. Add garlic and shallots and cook until transparent, stirring constantly.
7. Add larger mushrooms first (lobster, Portobello and king).
8. Sauté for 3 minutes, then add all other mushrooms.
9. Season with salt and pepper. Add more oil if mushrooms start to "dry" out. Cook for another 5 minutes.
10. Remove from the heat and allow the mushrooms to cool down until you can handle them. Rough chop the mixture and transfer it to a bowl.
11. Add the sour cream, mix well and taste.
12. Scoop or spread the fricassee onto the crostini.

INDEX